modern
women

First published in hardback in 2017 by Frances Lincoln,
an imprint of The Quarto Group.

The Old Brewery, 6 Blundell Street,
London, N7 9BH, United Kingdom.
www.QuartoKnows.com

This paperback edition first published in 2021 by Aurum

A catalogue record for this book is available from the British Library.

978-0-7112-5515-9

1 2 3 4 5 6 7 8 9 10

Cover design by Paileen Currie
Typeset in Gotham by SX Desktop Publishing
Printed and bound by CPI Group (UK) Ltd, Croydon, CR0 4YY

modern women

52 Pioneers who changed the World

Waterford City and County
Libraries

Kira Cochrane

Aurum

Contents

Alice Guy-Blaché

Film director, 1873–1968

Alice Guy-Blaché, 1913.

> *‛ There is nothing connected with the staging of a motion picture that a woman cannot do as easily as a man ’*

In 1914, Alice Guy-Blaché was perfectly clear. 'There is nothing connected with the staging of a motion picture,' she wrote, 'that a woman cannot do as easily as a man, and there is no reason why she cannot completely master every technicality of the art.'

Guy-Blaché had been directing films for almost 20 years by the time she wrote this, starting in France in 1896. She was one of the first people – perhaps the very first – to use narrative in film; also one of the first to shoot on location and to sync picture and sound; and she had pioneered essential techniques including double exposure and fadeouts. When she moved to the US in 1907, her success continued, only briefly abated by marriage, which traditionally ended women's careers in this era. While pregnant with her second child Reginald in 1912, she built a major studio, Solax, in New Jersey, costing the equivalent of millions of dollars today. It included prop rooms, carpentry shops, laboratories, darkrooms and projection rooms, everything necessary for a film industry that was rising from the dust.

Many of Guy-Blaché's films were ambitious and well reviewed, but for years her name was forgotten – she moved back to France in 1922, and on returning to the US in 1927, in search of her films, found nothing. Her work, and that of other pioneering female filmmakers, seemed lost forever. As the sound era began in the late 1920s, and film became increasingly big business, the woman director started to seem a mythical figure, as illustrated by the history of the Academy Award for Best Director. First awarded in the late 1920s, it wasn't until 2009 that the first woman won – Kathryn Bigelow for *The Hurt Locker* – by which time more than 400 men had been nominated, and only four women.

In the earliest days of Hollywood, women were at the forefront. Major directors included Lois Weber, Mabel Normand and Dorothy Arzner; Katharine Hepburn was directed by Arzner in the 1933 film *Christopher Strong*, and wrote in her autobiography *Me*, six decades later, 'it seems odd now, a woman director, but it didn't seem strange to me then', a reminder that progress is not always linear, and requires constant vigilance. Leading silent era screenwriters included Frances Marion and Anita Loos; Mary Pickford became famous for her dramatic roles, and women were among the first action stars, with Pearl White and Ruth Roland establishing themselves as the 'serial queens', a model for the athletic, tenacious new woman of the 1910s.

In 1915, film writer Robert Grau remarked, 'in no line of endeavour has a woman made so emphatic an impress than in the amazing film industry'. Grau is quoted in Anthony Slide's book *The Silent Feminists*, in which Slide makes the impressive claim that Guy-Blaché 'virtually single-handedly established the concept of the director as a separate entity in the film-making process'.

Her influence began in the mid-1890s, when she was working as the office manager at a company in Paris which specialised in still photography. Her boss, Léon Gaumont, was friends with the Lumière brothers, Auguste and Louis, who showed up one day and invited them to a screening of a movie they had made. Guy-Blaché was an avid reader, the daughter of a bookseller, and could see the potential for film to move beyond short documentary clips. She therefore suggested to Gaumont that she could write a few scenes, and ask her friends to perform them. 'If the future development of motion pictures had been foreseen at this time, I should never have obtained his consent,' she wrote in her memoir. 'My youth, my inexperience, my sex, all conspired against me.' But Guy-Blaché had foresight in her favour. Decades later, her daughter Simone remarked that Gaumont had dismissed the motion picture camera, the basis for the most influential art form of the twentieth century, as 'a child's toy'.

Guy-Blaché's first film, *La Fée aux Choux* (The Cabbage Fairy), was based on a French children's story, and shows a beautifully-dressed woman smiling and producing a baby from the leaves of a cabbage. From these slight beginnings, she directed hundreds of films, including melodramas, comedies, westerns and military features, with writer Karen Ward Mahar observing that Guy-Blaché 'promoted active female leads' – she directed five films, for instance, starring British vaudeville star Olga Petrova (born Muriel Harding), who insisted on playing dominant women. A couple of her films have clear feminist themes, including her 1906 comedy, *The Consequences of Feminism*. This shows traditional male and female roles reversed – men looking after children while women carouse in a bar – and though it has sometimes been read as a critique of feminism, it can perhaps more obviously be seen as a critique of male behaviour. Several scenes show a man being pressured into sex by a woman, pinpointing the problem of sexual harassment before that term even existed.

Slide has suggested Guy-Blaché's career was harmed by her husband, Herbert Blaché, who also directed films. She was unquestionably the better director, writes Slide, but her husband, 'routinely advertised himself and his services above those of his wife. On some films, Blaché would even insist that his wife take on the duties of his assistant director, which lowered her status in the film community'. Blaché was unfaithful, and it was when the pair separated in 1922, that Guy-Blaché returned to France.

She never regained a foothold in film making, but did eventually secure recognition for her work – more than a hundred of her films have now been rediscovered – and was awarded the Legion of Honour in 1953. 'Be natural' said a poster at her studio, a radical suggestion for early film performers, who were used to striking melodramatic poses. Guy-Blaché was a natural herself.

Tegla Loroupe

Marathon runner, b.1973

Tegla Loroupe waves to the crowd after winning the women's
10,000 metre race at the 1998 Goodwill Games.

> *'Of course people said I should
> stay home, not run, but I was
> not listening to them. Women
> always have to fight. Nothing
> is easy for us'*

Crossing the finish line of the New York marathon in 1995, coming first for the second time in two years, Tegla Loroupe began to sob. It had been an emotionally lacerating week. Phone calls to her home in Kenya from her training base in Germany had proved strangely evasive, she told *The New York Times*, until a neighbour let slip that her family was away at a funeral. They wouldn't say whose. After more phone calls it emerged that Loroupe's sister Albina had died of a stomach haemorrhage, aged 33, and their mother Mary passed on her deathbed message: 'I'm crossing my fingers for Tegla. Tell her to have courage and to fulfil her responsibility in New York.'

Loroupe's mother and sister had been encouraging her for years – Mary had grown up an orphan, and stressed the importance of independence, while Albina advised that she would only win the respect of men if she owned something substantial. As a small child, growing up with 24 siblings and half-siblings in a Kenyan village on the border with Uganda, Loroupe's chances of achieving this must have felt slight. Her father had four wives, and he expected his daughter to lead a traditional life, working on the family farm, marrying in her late teens and having children. He was not, at first, in favour of her education – her mother and Albina pushed for this – and when she was twelve and started attending a boarding school in the nearby town of Kapenguria, it was on the basis that she would concentrate on her studies. She was not allowed to run.

But the school authorities told her she would have to forgo her father's wishes. If she didn't agree to run, they would make her complete the school track on her knees. Without any gym kit, she began running in her blouse and skirt, and was soon the national high school champion in cross country and middle distance.

In her late teens, after college courses in accounting and a job with the Kenyan postal service, Loroupe travelled to Germany to start training in earnest. The effort paid off with her groundbreaking win in the New York marathon in 1994 – the first time a black African woman had won a major marathon. She was lauded when she returned to her home village. Women gave her livestock and land, told her how much she had encouraged them, and within a few years, more and more women in Kenya, and across Africa, were competing as runners. Loroupe's example changed the world of marathon and distance running for good.

Loroupe won marathons in London, Rome, Boston, Rotterdam, Hong Kong and Berlin, as well as New York, broke the record for this distance, and for 20, 25 and 30 kilometres. Her manager, Volker Wagner, once remarked of her internal drive, to *The New York Times*, 'it's like she is on a mission', and that propulsion didn't wane when she stopped running competitively.

Loroupe knew a success in that second New York marathon would fulfil her sudden responsibility to provide for her sister's six children. And this urge to provide for her community runs through her work. With resources scarce in the area where she grew up, there has been ongoing conflict between the various communities, and in 2003, she set up the Tegla Loroupe Peace Foundation, to try to resolve some of these old battles and bolster people's livelihoods. That same year, she began a series of peace races, bringing people from warring communities together to run; echoing the Olympic slogan, the motto of her organisation is 'peace through sports'. She has also set up a peace academy, for children who have been orphaned as a result of conflict or HIV/AIDS, and runs a training programme for refugee athletes.

Loroupe has supported and inspired countless women athletes. 'You'll be the best. You can take the pain,' her mother once remarked. Her daughter has proved her right, many times over.

Del Martin &
Phyllis Lyon

Lesbian activists, 1921–2008 & 1924–2020

Phyllis Lyon and Del Martin.

In the first issue of the lesbian magazine *The Ladder*, Del Martin wrote that 'nothing was ever accomplished by hiding in a dark corner'. The words proved prophetic for her and her great love, Phyllis Lyon, who dedicated their lives to gay rights in a truly perilous era.

Martin was writing in 1956, during a decade in the US which the writer Lillian Faderman has called 'perhaps the worst time in history for women to love women'. As Faderman describes in her book *Odd Girls and Twilight Lovers*, Senator Joseph McCarthy's communist witch hunt had been broadened to target gay people, and an atmosphere of intense suspicion and paranoia prevailed. There were police raids not just on gay and lesbian bars but on private parties too; people applying for 'sensitive' government jobs had to undergo a lie detector test regarding their sexual orientation; the women's army corp began using a verbal test for recruits, designed to weed out lesbians, which included the question 'do you envision sucking a woman's breast?'; and in 1955, the dean and assistant dean of students at the University of California, Los Angeles, co-authored an article recommending gay students be forced to leave college if they refused to commit to changing their sexuality. Some parents sent lesbian daughters to psychiatric hospitals, and very few gay people felt secure in their jobs. Many underwent 'front' marriages, marrying someone of the opposite sex, to divert suspicion.

It was not, in other words, an atmosphere in which anyone would have felt especially confident about starting a lesbian social club. But in 1955, Martin and Lyon became co-founders of The Daughters of Bilitis, the first lesbian organisation in the US, and soon began organising for gay rights. (Bilitis was a fictional lesbian contemporary of the poet Sappho, who appeared in Pierre Louÿs's 1894 poetry collection *The Songs of Bilitis*.) The group started secretive and small – as Lyon reflected years later, there was no way they could advertise in that punitive era – but their magazine *The Ladder* built up 500 subscribers, who shared it with friends, and chapters began from Chicago to Cleveland, Detroit to Denver. Daughters of Bilitis stressed to members and subscribers that their names would stay safe, out of the hands of the authorities – not realising the group had been infiltrated by informants, who were passing information to the FBI and CIA.

Martin and Lyon met in the early 1950s as journalists on the same trade newspaper in Seattle. At that stage Lyon had never heard the word 'lesbian' and was fascinated when Martin declared, in a bar one night, that she was one. They became friends, and when Lyon was preparing to leave her job at the paper, their relationship changed. 'What I always say is that we were sitting on the couch in my apartment,' Lyon told writer Laura Barton years later, 'and she made half a pass at me, and I had to make the other half, and then we had sex that night for the very first time, which was very interesting, and certainly very different than I had been used to with men. And more fun I think.'

On Valentine's Day in 1953, the pair moved into an apartment in the Castro district of San Francisco, and their extraordinary activist careers began. They helped found the Council on Religion and the Homosexual in 1964, which organised against discriminatory laws, and in the early 1970s they started working with the Alice B Toklas Democratic Club, which campaigns for political candidates who are supportive of gay rights.

They also became involved with the feminist movement. Martin was the first open lesbian elected to the board of the National Organisation for Women (NOW), at a time when one of its founders, the highly influential writer Betty Friedan, author of feminist classic *The Feminine Mystique* (1963), considered gay women 'the lavender menace'. (Friedan went so far, writes Faderman, as to announce in *The New York Times* in 1973 that lesbians were part of a plot to discredit feminism, and had been sent to infiltrate the movement by the CIA.) Thankfully, other feminists were more open-minded, and Lyon and Martin encouraged the passing of a NOW resolution in 1971, which recognised lesbian rights.

The pair spearheaded a successful campaign for homo-sexuality to be removed from the American Psychiatric Association's roster of mental illnesses in 1973, and wrote books together – *Lesbian/Woman* (1972) and *Lesbian Love and Liberation* (1973). Martin also wrote *Battered Wives* (1976), an analysis of misogyny and domestic violence.

But perhaps the most visible of all their activism came in their later years, as part of the drive for equal marriage. In February 2004, the pair were the first gay couple to be married in San Francisco, after the mayor ordered the city clerk to start handing out same sex marriage licenses. When the mayor's decision was overturned by the California Supreme Court, exactly six months later, and their marriage was voided, Martin and Lyon became plaintiffs in a series of lawsuits which led to the ban being overturned. In June 2008, when Lyon was 83 and Martin was 87, just two months before Martin's death, they once again became the first gay couple to be married in San Francisco, making manifest the feminist slogan 'the personal is political' in one last perfect moment of love and activism.

Mary Anning
Palaeontologist, 1799–1847

Mary Anning, painted by an unknown artist, c. 1842.

> *'And what is a woman? Was she not made of the same flesh and blood as lordly Man? Yes, and was destined doubtless, to become his friend, his helpmate on his pilgrimage but surely not his slave, for is not reason Hers?'*

One freezing night in December 1823, Mary Anning was at the foot of a cliff near her home in Lyme Regis, working to free her discovery from the earth. It was the skeleton of a nine foot long creature, with four paddles and a tiny head, an almost complete example of an ancient marine reptile of which she had found a partial skeleton a few years earlier.

The discovery of a Plesiosaurus was the latest in a series of finds which started before Anning reached adulthood. In 1812, a year after Anning's older brother Joseph found the skull of an Ichthyosaurus, she found its skeleton – the first complete skeleton of what would later be renamed Temnodontosaurus platyodon. She was just twelve years old. The industries open to working class women were farm labour, domestic service and the emerging field of factory work, but Anning pursued a different course, exploring the remarkably fossil-rich coastline of Lyme Regis for bones that profoundly expanded our understanding of the world and its origins. Mary Anning is 'probably the most important unsung (or inadequately sung) collecting force in the history of palaeontology,' wrote Stephen Jay Gould in 1992. 'She directly found, or pointed the way to, nearly every specimen of importance.'

Born in 1799, Anning's prospects seemed bleak; Richard and Molly Anning had nine children, and only Mary and Joseph survived infancy. These were particularly hard times for poor families, as Patricia Pierce writes in the biography, *Jurassic Mary*, and a year after Anning was born, her father Richard, a cabinet-maker, led a bread riot in Lyme, protesting against the scarcity of food. Richard was a dissenter, a religious non-conformist, who attended the Congregationalist church, rather than the Church of England. This was not unusual in Lyme, but was controversial in the wider world, giving the family an outsider status.

Anning learned to read and write at the Dissenters' Sunday school she attended from the age of eight, and a copy of a religious magazine given to her by her brother survives – it contains essays on two subjects that would define her life's work, one reasserting the Genesis story that God created the earth in six days and rested on the seventh, the other encouraging dissenters to learn about the new field of geology (which would call that Bible teaching into question). As children, she and Joseph went on fossil-finding expeditions with their father, selling small finds on a table outside their home.

In 1810, Richard died of consumption, aged 44, and the family was left in debt. Anning's finds showed an entrepreneurial as well as a scientific streak, with that first discovery of a seventeen foot ichthyosaur, when she was twelve, sold to the Lord of the Manor for £23. In 1826, Anning and her mother Molly opened a shop where they sold fossils, bones and sea shells, and in 1844 Dr Carus, the King of Saxony's medical attendant, described a visit. 'We fell in with a shop in which the most remarkable petrifactions and fossil remains – the head of an Ichthyosaurus, beautiful ammonites, etc, were exhibited in the window,' he wrote.

Anning's search for fossils was often dangerous, notes Pierce. The best discoveries were made when the weather was turbulent, the ground unstable, bones rising to the earth's surface; on one expedition, Anning came close to being killed by a falling rock, which killed her beloved dog Tray instead. By the age of 30, she had made five major discoveries – including a Pterodactylus macronyx in 1828 (later named the Dimorphodon macronyx) – and had honed her ability, not just in the extraction, preservation, presentation and sketching of the bones, but in investigating them. She became skilled at dissecting existing creatures, comparing their anatomy to that of their prehistoric forbears.

This was not a good era in which to be a female scientist – particularly one of a working class, dissenter background. The Royal Society of London, founded in 1660, didn't elect women fellows until 1945, and Anning wasn't even allowed to attend meetings of the Geological Society, let alone become a fellow. As a result, it was geologist William Buckland, rather than her, who lectured to the society in 1829 about Anning's discovery of the Pterodactylus macronyx. This was the same Buckland who, in 1831, on becoming president of the British Association for the Advancement of Science, explained that members had decided to keep women out, because if they were to attend, 'it would at once turn the thing into a sort of Albemarle-dilettante-meeting, instead of a serious philosophical union of working men'.

That same year, Anna Maria Pinney wrote about her friend Anning's bitterness: 'according to her these men of learning have sucked her brains, and made a great deal by publishing works, of which she furnished the contents, while she derived none of the advantages.' Anning had every reason to be angry. For all her brilliant discoveries, her life was marked by poverty and loneliness, and came to an early end, when she was just 47 years old. She had suffered the pain of breast cancer for at least two years.

After her death her contribution began to be celebrated, starting with a tribute by her friend Henry De La Beche, president of the Geological Society, to gathered members – it was the first time a woman had been paid tribute there. Charles Dickens published an essay about her in his periodical *All the Year Round*, in 1865, ending with the line 'the carpenter's daughter has won a name for herself, and has deserved to win it'.

More recently, the Natural History Museum has called Anning, 'the greatest fossil hunter ever known'. This all came too late, of course. But, as with Anning's discoveries, her name has survived the vagaries of time.

Katie Sandwina

Circus strong woman, 1884–1952

Katie Sandwina in her performing costume.

In March 1912, the Barnum and Bailey circus formed a group to campaign for women's suffrage. It was launched at the menagerie room at Madison Square Garden, reported the *New York Tribune*, where 'elephants trumpeted and got all tangled up in their chains and a man-eating hyena peeked out of his cage and grinned'; the afternoon's events included a baby giraffe being christened Miss Suffrage. With around 25 circus women in attendance, including acrobats, animal trainers and wire walkers, it closed with a rallying cry from long-time bareback rider Josie De Mott Robinson. 'You earn salaries,' she told the gathered women. 'Some of you have property. You have a right to say what shall be done with it. You want to establish clearly in the mind of your husband that you are his equal.'

One woman who presumably had very little trouble convincing anyone that she was her husband's equal was Katie Sandwina, vice president of the suffrage group, and the circus's resident strong woman. In her essential essay, 'Centre Ring: Katie Sandwina and the Construction of Celebrity', Jan Todd writes that Sandwina had met her husband, acrobat Max Heymann, while performing in Saxony around the turn of the century, after challenging audience members to a wrestling match, with a prize for whoever could beat her. Heymann volunteered and was duly trounced, but he rode off with Sandwina's affection. In accounts of the circus suffrage meeting it was reported that one man, a bareback rider, had interrupted, ordering his wife home to make him dinner. The strong woman faced no such humiliation. 'Mrs Sandwina is usually photographed in the act of tossing several persons about,' reported *The New York Times*, 'and one moment in her act catches her in the easy task of lifting into the air an iron bar with four full-grown persons hanging [from] it. Mr Sandwina did not interrupt yesterday's meeting.'

In the Barnum and Bailey circus, as well as lifting her husband and other men above her head, Sandwina reportedly carried a 600 pound cannon on her back, juggled cannon balls and bent iron bars. One reporter was moved to remark that those who opposed women's right to the vote would tremble on seeing her lift, with one arm, her husband and two-year-old son, who the press called 'Superbaby'. 'When all women are able to rule their homes by such simple and primitive methods they will get the vote – or take it,' the reporter continued. Journalists called her Sandwina the Suffragette.

It might be thought that a circus strong woman was a draw primarily because she was considered freakish – and certainly, Sandwina's strength was unusual. But one of the most interesting aspects of the coverage was its frank focus on her beauty. Todd quotes an interview conducted by Kate Carew, one of the best known journalists of the era. 'She is as majestic as the Sphinx,' wrote Carew, 'as pretty as a valentine, as sentimental as a German schoolgirl, and as wholesome as a great big slice of bread and butter.' Sandwina's physique was also described in glowing terms by contemporaries. Robert Fellows, head of publicity for the circus, organised a press conference to introduce Sandwina, during which she was examined by doctors. Her measurements came in at almost five foot ten inches, 210 pounds, a 44-inch chest, 29-inch waist, 43-inch hips and a bicep that expanded to fourteen inches when flexed. According to the doctors, this made her, 'a perfect woman by all the accepted standards', her size and strength publicly venerated.

Sandwina was born Katharina Brumbach in or just outside Vienna to a family of Bavarian circus performers – her father Philippe could reputedly lift 500 pounds with one finger, while her mother Johanna performed as a strong woman when not looking after her fifteen or sixteen children, of whom Sandwina was the second. As a child, Sandwina began building her strength, and her emergence as an icon of female power came during what's now some-times called the first wave of feminism, an era in the West when more and more women were entering the workplace and higher education, and finding new freedom riding bicycles and flying aeroplanes. This was the age of the New Woman, the battle for the women's vote was being waged in countries around the world, and women were fighting, too, for sexual and bodily autonomy, and equality with men. This gave an added potency to the images that appeared on Sandwina's posters, showing her, for instance, holding a dumbbell on which the weight consisted of a man at each end.

In the years after Sandwina's greatest celebrity, the fashion for strong women waned, and, as Gloria Steinem writes in her essay 'The Politics of Muscle', the idealised female form has instead veered between fecundity and thinness. 'Whenever a patriarchy wants females to populate a new territory or replenish an old one, big breasts and hips become admirable,' writes Steinem, citing the Marilyn Monroe-type figure popular in post-war western societies. 'As soon as increased population wasn't desirable or necessary, hips and breasts were de-emphasised. Think of the Twiggy look that arrived in the 1960s'.

Women's bodies have always been shaped by social pressures, and female weakness has often been encouraged, and reinforced by the denigration of muscular sports women, and the celebration of fashion images in which, in some cases, women seem barely strong enough to stand. It wasn't until 2000 that women's weightlifting was included at the Olympics, 104 years after the men's event began. But in the meantime, there was Katie Sandwina, pictured on a plinth emblazoned with the words 'the wonder of female strength', holding three men on a bicycle above her head.

Billie Jean King

Tennis player, b.1943

Billie Jean King in action against Bobby Riggs, September 1973.

> *'Pressure is a privilege*
> *– it only comes to those*
> *who earn it'*

The most-watched match of Billie Jean King's career was one of the most-watched matches in tennis history, and it wasn't played on a court at Wimbledon, the French Open, or any other major tournament; it wasn't against any of the other great women players of the era; it wasn't a match, in fact, that King wanted to play at all.

Earlier that year, 1973, Bobby Riggs, who had been the number one male tennis player in his heyday, had taken on Margaret Court, who was number one in the women's game at the time. He was 55, she was 30, and he beat her in straight sets, 6-2 6-1, in what became known as the Mother's Day Massacre. The second wave feminist movement in the US was burgeoning, and the defeat gave chauvinists the perfect chance to attack women with their weapon of choice: ridicule.

Riggs was a gambler and hustler, and he had been pushing to play King all along; in his flamboyant, slightly ludicrous style, he called her 'the sex leader of the revolutionary pack'. He was right to see her as a leader. The daughter of a homemaker mother and firefighter father, King had started playing tennis aged eleven, on the public courts of Long Beach, California, and by the time she was twelve, she knew she didn't just want to dominate the game, but to change it. 'I looked around,' she told me in an interview for the *Guardian* in 2013, 'and I saw that everyone who plays wears white socks, white shoes, a white tennis dress or shorts, and they're all white. My question to myself, as a twelve-year-old, was: where is everybody else? There are no people of colour. Something's not right'.

Her tenacity on the court was extraordinary. During her sporting career, she won 39 Grand Slam titles in singles, women's doubles and mixed doubles. But her tenacity off the court was perhaps even more remarkable.

She started playing internationally in 1961, when she was seventeen, and was one of the players who pushed successfully for the game to become 'open', for professionals and amateurs to be able to compete together. This meant players could earn a living. When King won three titles at Wimbledon in 1967, the year before the open era started, her total prize was a £45 gift voucher. In 1968, when she won the Wimbledon singles title for the third time (she would win it six times in all), she received £750.

That was a huge improvement, but it paled beside the £2,000 that the men's winner, Rod Laver, had taken home, and in other tennis competitions the pay differential was even bigger, the men's purse up to twelve times the women's purse. A professional organisation was being formed by the male players, to protect their interests, and when King asked if women could join, she was told 'absolutely not . . . Nobody would even pay a dime to watch you girls'.

She and eight other players started a women's tour, despite being told by the US Lawn Tennis Association, as it was then, that they would be suspended from other competitions, including Wimbledon and the US Open. The tour was a hit, the women kept playing in major competitions, and they soon formed their own professional body, the Women's Tennis Association, with King as its first president. The early 1970s were also spent campaigning for the legislation that would become Title IX, which outlawed sexual discrimination in the provision of federal assistance for educational programs – meaning women athletes in the US began receiving college scholarships alongside their male peers. This led to a 622 per cent increase in the number of female college athletes.

All this had been achieved in the years leading up to King's showdown with Riggs, and a defeat would jeopardise everything. But the scoreboard of the Mother's Day Massacre left King feeling she had little choice – she couldn't leave it unchallenged. She braced herself for what would prove one of the great spectacles of the women's movement, a game dubbed The Battle of the Sexes.

It started with an exchange of gifts: Riggs gave her a lollipop, she handed him a piglet. The scene was comical, but the pressure was serious. The worldwide TV audience numbered 100 million.

King faltered in the first games, but then began playing from the baseline, sending shots to Riggs that forced him to run all over the court. The tactic worked. She won in straight sets, 6–4, 6–3, 6–3, and when the match ended Riggs jumped over the net and told her 'I underestimated you'.

The pressure had been intensified by the tumult in her personal life. King married her husband Larry in 1965, but realised in the late 1960s that she had feelings for women, and began an affair a few years afterwards with her personal assistant Marilyn Barnett. This reached the public eye in 1981, after the affair had ended, when Barnett sued her for palimony. The courts ruled in King's favour, but she immediately lost all her endorsements and was forced to postpone her retirement from professional tennis, playing simply to pay the lawyers.

King weathered this, and began campaigning for gay rights. In 1975, *Sports Illustrated* had declared it very likely she would 'go down in history as the most significant athlete of this century' and the tribute Barack Obama paid her, on awarding her the presidential medal of freedom in 2009, confirms how well she lived up to that epiphany, aged twelve. 'Today,' said Obama, 'we honour what she calls "all the off-the-court stuff" – what she did to broaden the reach of the game, to change how women athletes and women everywhere view themselves, and to give everyone, regardless of gender or sexual orientation – including my two daughters – a chance to compete both on the court and in life.'

Kathleen Hanna

Singer, b.1968

Kathleen Hanna performing with Bikini Kill at the Rock for Choice
concert in Los Angeles, California, April 1993.

> *'Feminism isn't something that you are, it's something that you do'*

In 1991, in the second issue of the *Bikini Kill* zine, Kathleen Hanna published her riot grrrl manifesto. The revolution she had in mind would save the psychic and cultural lives of girls and women everywhere, she wrote, and help them gather the strength and community to address racism, classism and sexism. She ended with her belief that girls constituted a revolutionary force 'that can and will change the world for real'.

Hanna had the energy to power a new movement. Byher late teens, while studying at Evergreen State College in Olympia, Washington, she had interned at a domestic violence shelter, put on her own art show at college – and, after the show was censored, started a gallery with friends. She had also begun performing spoken word pieces, one of which provides the opening scene of the documentary *The Punk Singer* (2013), directed by Sini Anderson. It's Olympia, 1991, and Hanna is speaking/shouting: 'I'm your worst nightmare come to life, because I'm not going to shut up. I'm going to tell everyone'.

Attending a workshop with avant-garde writer Kathy Acker, Hanna told her of this determination to speak out. As related in Sara Marcus's essential riot grrrl history, *Girls to the Front*, Acker asked why she was doing spoken word. 'I feel like my whole life no one's ever listened to me,' said Hanna. 'I want people to listen'. There was more of a community for musicians than writers, said Acker. She should really start a band.

Hanna started several. She was singer and keyboardist for a group called Amy Carter, then front woman for Viva Knievel, writing songs primarily about sexual assault. On reading *Jigsaw*, a zine by fellow Olympia punk Tobi Vail, she was inspired by the comment, 'I've always been interested in playing music with other women. And it seems like I've always been misunderstood and gotten called sexist for it'. Hanna sent Vail a series of interviews she'd written, conversations with musicians, and they became friends, moving into next door apartments, discussing the movement Vail called the Revolution Girl Style Now.

There had been feminist punk bands in the 1970s, British groups including The Slits, The Raincoats, and X-Ray Spex, fronted by young singer Poly Styrene, who was known for her shouted, growling refrain, 'Oh bondage, up yours!' Punk was a starting point too for some of the biggest 1980s US girl bands, including The Go-Gos. But by the time Vail and Hanna met, the punk scene was overwhelmingly male, and gigs could be an ordeal, with girls forced to the sidelines to avoid the violence and wandering hands of the mosh pit.

Vail named the band Bikini Kill and they began practising in Autumn 1990. 'I remember being nervous,' Hanna told Marcus, years later, 'but thinking I was on a total fucking mission, so I was just gonna fake my way through this "being in a band" thing.' Early footage shows Hanna jumping up and down, or marching on the spot, ordering the girls in the crowd to the front, off the sidelines.

Other bands started, including Bratmobile and Heavens to Betsy, and in July 1991, the movement had its name, with the first issue of the zine *Riot Grrrl*, put together by Hanna, Allison Wolfe and Molly Neuman of Bratmobile, and their friend Jen Smith, who said there needed to be a girl riot. The second half of the name, Marcus writes, was 'the growling "grrrl" spelling that Tobi had recently made up as a jokey variation on all the tortured spellings of "womyn/womon/ wimmin" feminists liked to experiment with'.

Riot grrrl chapters began, with meetings which reflected the consciousness-raising discussions of the 1970s, women speaking publicly about their experience of sexual assault, rape and abortion, realising these were collective experiences, and might therefore have political solutions. The movement grew out of Olympia's DIY culture, the notion you could pick up a guitar or a pen and begin creating, and girls started their own bands, zines, and held riot grrrl conventions – feminism had always been good at critiquing art and culture, not always so good at making it. Riot grrrl began in the UK, where the band Huggy Bear protested against sexism on late-night TV show *The Word*, bringing feminism into the mainstream.

The 1970s feminist movement had been pushed down by forces Susan Faludi unpicked in her 1991 bestseller *Backlash: The Undeclared War Against Women*. In the US, abortion rights were under threat, violence against women persisted, and the Christian right was increasingly influential, with Pat Robertson, a former candidate for the Republican presidential nomination, describing feminism as 'a socialist, anti-family political movement that encourages women to leave their husbands, kill their children, practice witchcraft, destroy capitalism and become lesbians'. The media referred a lot to post-feminism, suggesting the movement had been and gone. Meanwhile, the sexism feminists had attacked was back – sometimes blatant, sometimes draped in a gauzy veil of irony.

Bikini Kill broke up on friendly terms in the late 1990s – but their influence continued, first in the depoliticised girl power of the Spice Girls, then in the highly politicised punk fury of Pussy Riot. Hanna formed feminist party band Le Tigre, but left in 2005, when she became increasingly sick with a strange, debilitating illness. It was years before a diagnosis of late stage Lyme disease prompted long, intensive treatment.

Hanna's band The Julie Ruin, formed in 2010, built on the album, *Julie Ruin*, which she recorded in her bedroom in 1997, using a $40 drum machine. 'Girls' bedrooms sometimes can be this space of real creativity,' she said of that album. 'The problem is that these bedrooms are all cut off from each other.' In her willingness to get up and make something, to take the risk, Hanna told a generation of girls they could do it too.

Harriet Tubman

Abolitionist, c.1822–1913

Harriet Tubman, c. 1885.

In 1849, Harriet Tubman decided she would escape slavery, whatever it took. The man who owned her had just died and her future was more uncertain than ever. Would she be sold to another family? Forced to leave her relatives and husband? At the mercy of the cruelest market, she made a resolution: 'There was one of two things I had a right to, liberty or death; if I could not have one, I would have the other.'

Tubman became one of the most famous fugitives in the history of slavery. She ended up saving hundreds of other enslaved people through her work on the Underground Railroad (UGRR) – a secret network of abolitionists who helped spirit fugitives to safety – as well as a daring raid she led along the Combahee River during the American Civil War.

She was born Araminta Ross, to enslaved couple Harriet Green and Benjamin Ross, and spent her early years on a plantation in Maryland. Her working life began aged five, when a local woman employed her to take care of a baby. As Catherine Clinton writes in her biography of Tubman, she was so small she had to sit on the floor to safely cradle the child. Her day was filled with domestic chores, and at night she had to ensure the baby didn't wake anyone – if she failed, she was whipped, and there were once five whippings before breakfast, leaving her with lifelong scars.

Tubman was returned to her mother, then hired out to another family. Still a small child, she was so scared of this new mistress that when she was caught eating a sugar lump, she fled, hiding in a pig pen from Friday until Tuesday, fighting the pigs for potato peelings. It was an impossible existence, negotiated with sad ingenuity. While living with one particularly brutal mistress, she took to wearing as many thick clothes as she could, as protection from the beatings.

In early adolescence, when Tubman was working in the fields, a row broke out between the overseer and a field hand, and Tubman intervened. A lead weight thrown by the overseer hit her and, as she later said, 'broke my skull'. She began to experience what, to modern eyes, might be diagnosed as narcolepsy, falling into sudden, deep sleep.

In 1844, she married free man, John Tubman, and not long afterwards hired a lawyer to investigate her mother's status – she had an inkling her mother might be legally free. She discovered her mother had been kept in slavery for more than a decade beyond the date she should have been freed, and some of her siblings had likely been born free. Her resolve to escape deepened.

Tubman set off alone in September 1849, making the ninety mile journey to Philadelphia on foot, helped by members of the underground railroad, the 'conductors' and 'stationmasters', who assisted fugitive slaves to escape their owners, providing hiding places and showing the route to the next safe spot. This was a serious risk for all involved.

Rewards were often offered for fugitive slaves, and posses hunted them with bloodhounds – a notice in the Cambridge Democrat on 3 October 1849 offered $50 for 'MINTY, aged about 27 years' if Tubman was found within state lines, $100 if she had crossed into another state. Clinton writes that some slave owners cut the Achilles tendons of those who had tried to escape, while others branded them.

Tubman renamed herself Harriet on reaching Philadelphia, and might have been expected simply to enjoy her liberation; the passing of the Fugitive Slave Law in 1850 – known to abolitionists as the Bloodhound Law – would have deterred most fugitives from ever passing into a slave state again. But Tubman decided to return to Maryland, as an 'abductor' for the UGRR. Many of those involved with the railroad were white male abolitionists. As an African-American woman and fugitive slave, Tubman was taking a colossal risk.

On mission after mission, she was never caught, and never lost one of the people she helped to free. In moments of danger, she was quick thinking. When walking close to her former home in Maryland, she disguised herself with a large bonnet, and brought a couple of chickens with her – approached by a former master, she pulled a string attached to the chickens' legs, and their squawking created a diversion. An encounter with another previous master was averted when she picked up a newspaper. Known to be illiterate, this disguised her identity.

Tubman undertook around thirteen missions in eight years, leading approximately 70 people to freedom, including her own parents. (When she tried to convince her husband to follow her to Philadelphia, it emerged he had started a relationship with another woman.)

Her heroism didn't stop with the UGRR. During the American Civil War, she worked as a nurse, and a spy, and became the first woman to lead an armed assault in that conflict. On 2 June 1863, Tubman led Union troops in three steamboats along the Combahee River, and, as the boat whistles sounded, hundreds of people ran towards them, recognising their chance for liberation. More than 750 were freed from slavery, an achievement remembered in the name of the influential 1970s black feminist lesbian organisation, the Combahee River Collective.

Tubman was lauded by abolitionists, and celebrated for her campaigning for women's suffrage. But she struggled with poverty, and battled to secure a war widow's pension after the death of her second husband Nelson Davis in 1888. She set up a home in Auburn, New York, for elderly African-Americans, and in her final years, moved in herself. As Clinton notes, her legacy lives on in the thousands of descendants of those she freed.

Vesta Tilley

Male impersonator, 1864–1952

Vesta Tilley, c. 1904.

What purpose did the male impersonators of the music halls fulfil for their female audiences? These acts, including Bessie Bonehill, Hetty King, Ella Shields and Vesta Tilley, grew popular in the UK and US in the late nineteenth and early twentieth centuries, when women were pushing for greater autonomy and equality with men, and they offered an intimation that gender roles were mutable, that stereotypes of femininity and masculinity could potentially be subverted. They offered, in other words, a blueprint for freedom (played out through comic songs). Gender stereotypes were so rigid that when Tilley appeared in a suit at the Royal Command performance of 1912, Queen Mary and the other ladies reportedly hid their faces behind their programmes, to protect themselves from seeing another woman's legs in trousers.

These acts also provided an outlet for hidden or suppressed desires, male and female. On occasion, when Tilley was singing in the guise of a dandy or a military man, a male voice would ring out from the audience, expressing his love. Was this admiration for the male character Tilley was playing, or for Tilley herself? The ambiguity made her even more popular with women, who were her most enthusiastic fans. As Tilley wrote in her autobiography, 'girls of all ages would wait in crowds to see me enter or leave the theatre, and each post brought piles of letters, varying from an impassioned declaration of undying love to a request for an autograph, or a photograph, or a simple flower, or a piece of ribbon I had worn'. One of her most fervent admirers produced a diary filled with expressions of devotion.

In Sara Maitland's 1986 biography of Tilley, she suggests the music hall star found the attentions of such women risible. She always emphasised her femininity off stage and when performing she was pointedly introduced as 'Miss Vesta Tilley' before launching into songs such as 'Jolly Good Luck to the Girl who Loves a Soldier' (with its refrain: 'Girls! If you'd like to love a soldier you can all love me!').

Born Matilda Powles in 1864, Tilley's life on stage began when she was a small child, the second of thirteen children. Nothing is known about her mother, but her father Harry Powles performed as a 'tramp musician' alongside their family dog Fatso, and in 1867 became chairman of the Theatre Royal in Gloucester, before moving on to manage St George's Music Hall in Nottingham. His daughter was under pressure to perform from the age of five, writes Maitland – she never went to school – and it was when she was around eight that she first appeared on stage dressed as the popular tenor Sim Reeves, performing the Victorian hit, 'Come Into the Garden Maud'. Soon she was earning £12 a week, and by the age of ten she was supporting her entire family.

By the second half of the 1890s, when Tilley was in her early thirties, she was thought to be the most highly paid working woman in Britain. This was the period when she conquered the US, her performances playing to packed audiences in New York, with male fans emulating the grey morning coat she wore to play a dandy and copying the ribbons she wore at one performance, in lieu of forgotten cufflinks. She licensed merchandise including her own straw boater, a waistcoat, socks and cigars, and appeared in a silent film alongside Stan Laurel and Charlie Chaplin. Her light mockery of the wealthy endeared her to working class audiences, and her light mockery of men endeared her to women.

In 1919, the year her husband Walter de Frece was knighted for his contribution to the war effort, Vesta Tilley began a year-long farewell tour, before retiring as Lady de Frece. She had been one of the most well known, and most financially powerful women in the country, but as Maitland notes, after her retirement she was moved to suggest women weren't well suited to public life. Tilley was not, we can surmise, an ardent feminist. But inadvertently, and powerfully, she opened up new space for female advancement – and female desire.

Leymah Gbowee

Peace activist, b.1972

Leymah Gbowee in New York, 2015.

> *'Using shared personal revelation to organise was completely new, and over time, it became one of the reasons our movement grew strong'*

'Gather the women to pray for peace'. Leymah Gbowee heard these words in a dream, after falling asleep in her office. When she woke at 5am, shaking, the phrase seemed to echo around her. 'It was like hearing the voice of God, yes, but . . . that wasn't possible,' she writes in her 2011 memoir, *Mighty Be Our Powers*. 'I drank too much. I fornicated! I was sleeping with a man who wasn't my husband, who in fact was still legally married to someone else. If God were going to speak to someone in Liberia, it wouldn't be to me!'

This revelation came more than ten years after civil war had broken out in her home country. In 1989, when Gbowee was seventeen, a happy high school graduate embarking on her degree, Charles Taylor and his rebels crossed in to Liberia, determined to overthrow the president of almost a decade, Samuel Doe. The country descended into chaos, with Doe, Taylor and other breakaway rebels stirring and exploiting ethnic tensions, Gbowee writes. She and her family had to leave their home, to find sanctuary, and it was while staying in a church compound that she saw a boy shot in front of her, heard stories of family friends being raped, and came to recognise the smell wafting over from a nearby beach. Executions were taking place, the bodies left to rot.

Almost a thousand people eventually took refuge in the church, and one day a government battalion arrived. 'Among the pews where we sang and prayed. . .' writes Gbowee, 'they raped, slashed, shot and hacked.' Outside, she saw children, babies and pregnant women among the dead.

In her twenties, Gbowee became a mother of four, and a social worker specialising in trauma healing. She spent more than two years working with the young men who had been child rebels under Taylor, some of whom had become fighters aged eight, and were discarded when they were injured, before picking out lives in abandoned buildings, begging, alone, considered contemptible. She worked too with the country's female security personnel, to help them envision their role as protectors of the people, rather than exploiters. There were meetings where the women talked about what they had seen, sharing stories of rape, violence, the death of their children. These conversations proved revelatory.

The discussions continued at the first meeting of the Women in Peacebuilding Network, in Accra in 2001, involving women from nearly all the sixteen West African nations. The network's founder, Thelma Ekiyor, chose Gbowee as a co-ordinator, and she threw herself into the work. In Liberia, where Charles Taylor was now in power, and the people lived in fear, Christian and Muslim women began organising together for peace. For six months they went to mosques, churches and markets, encouraging women to organise, handing out flyers that read: 'WE ARE TIRED OF OUR CHILDREN BEING KILLED! WE ARE TIRED

OF BEING RAPED! WOMEN, WAKE UP – YOU HAVE A VOICE IN THE PEACE PROCESS!'

In December 2002, 200 women marched along Tubman Boulevard in the nation's capital, Monrovia, singing Muslim songs and Christian hymns. Gbowee read out a message from a fellow campaigner: 'We envision peace. A peaceful coexistence that fosters equality, collective ownership and full participation of particularly women in all decision-making processes for conflict prevention.'

It was thirteen years since the start of the war, and another wave of violence began, a new breakaway rebel group taking towns and villages in the south-east of the country, people fleeing their homes for the poverty of the refugee camps. The women's peace network decided to make a public statement on the steps of the Monrovia city hall on 11 April 2003. Hundreds of women, all dressed in white, demanded an immediate, unconditional ceasefire and talks between the government and the rebels.

Thousands of women began gathering each day on a field nearby, sitting in the punishing heat, in silent protest. This was the start of the Mass Action for Peace. The women declared a sex strike – great for publicity, Gbowee said later – and when peace talks were called in Ghana, she and other members of the group went as delegates.

As the talks unfolded, over a couple of months, violence continued in Liberia, and Gbowee's optimism faltered. One day, as the negotiating hall filled with government officials and representatives from other Liberian political parties, she gathered 200 women and barricaded the exit. She passed a note to the man in charge of the talks, which said, 'We are holding these delegates, especially the Liberians, hostage. They will feel the pain of what our people are feeling at home.'

A security guard accused Gbowee of obstructing justice, and she was so angry that she began to strip. 'I was beside myself, desperate. . .' she writes in her memoir. 'These negotiations had been my last hope, but they were crashing, too. But in threatening to strip, I had summoned up a traditional power. In Africa, it's a terrible curse to see a married or elderly woman deliberately bare herself.' She was stopped by the official in charge of the talks, but her intervention seemed to work. The talks proceeded at a new pace, and not long afterwards Taylor resigned the presidency.

Gbowee faced personal difficulties as the war years unfolded. She felt trapped, for years, with a violent partner; she used alcohol, at times, as an escape; she was separated from her children for long periods, while working to support the family; and relationships within the women's peace movement were not always peaceful. The problems of daily life aren't superseded by conflict, but continue alongside it, and despite all this, it is sometimes possible to make a difference – even to help stop a war. In 2011, Gbowee was awarded the Nobel Peace Prize.

Valentina Tereshkova

Cosmonaut, b.1937

Valentina Tereshkova in Moscow, December 1966.

> *'Anyone who has spent any time in space will love it for the rest of their lives. I achieved my childhood dream of the sky'*

On 12 April 1961, Valentina Tereshkova caught the space bug. That day, Yuri Gagarin became the first person to break the bonds of the earth, and Tereshkova and her colleagues gathered around the radio, listening without breathing. When the programme ended they broke into laughter and shouting. Tereshkova's feelings were chaotic, she told the journal *Quest*, years later. She 'started to feel some nervousness, some shy thoughts . . . And then I decided. I'll be a cosmonaut'. Not long afterwards, she wrote to the Soviet authorities, volunteering to go into space, one of thousands of Soviet citizens to do so.

The odds on Tereshkova following Gagarin weren't obviously auspicious. While the first astronauts in the Soviet Union and the US were members of the military, Tereshkova was a civilian, with no background in science or engineering. In fact, she worked in a textile factory and had left school at sixteen. But the most glaring strike against her was that she was a woman. There were genuine arguments at the time as to whether a woman's body and mind could withstand space. As Tereshkova told *Quest*, some doctors and scientists believed, 'that in certain ways a female body is stronger and more able to survive than a male one. Others were convinced of the opposite.'

There were a few factors in her favour too. One was her membership of a parachuting club, where she had undertaken her first jump in 1959, and many more since. It was Gagarin's membership of a similar club which first convinced Tereshkova she might go into space, with parachuting an essential skill for the Soviet cosmonauts – while the first US space capsules landed in the sea, the Soviets had to bail out at 10,000 feet above the earth. After launching the first man into space, the Soviets were also keen to stay ahead of the US in the space race. As the head of the cosmonaut training programme, Lieutenant General Kamamin wrote in his diary: 'Under no circumstances should an American become the first woman in space – this would be an insult of Soviet women.'

In December 1961, Tereshkova was one of five women chosen for the space programme, out of thousands of volunteers, and entered intensive training at the Star City facility, outside Moscow. As Stephanie Nolen writes in *Promised the Moon: The Untold Story of the First Women in the Space Race*, Tereshkova was told to keep this a secret from her mother. As a cover, she said she was training for the national parachute team.

At Star City, there were flight simulations, isolation training, parachute jumps and classes in engineering and astronomy. Finally, in May 1963, Tereshkova learned she had been chosen, and just a month later, on 16 June, she embarked on her flight in the Vostok 6. Her codename was 'chaika' (seagull), and not long after launch, her voice rang out over Moscow Radio, to millions of Soviets: 'Here is Seagull. Everything is fine. I see the horizon; it's a sky blue with a dark strip. I see the earth. Everything is in order. I'm feeling fine. The machine is working well.'

This last statement wasn't true. Decades later, Tereshkova revealed that, soon after take off, she had discovered a serious, horrifying problem – the capsule was programmed to ascend, but not to descend. If the problem wasn't fixed, she would spin out ceaselessly into space. Thankfully, a new computer programme was installed, in orbit, and she promised not to breathe a word, to ensure the engineer responsible went unpunished. She kept the promise for 30 years.

Tereshkova spent two days, 22 hours and 50 minutes in space – more time than all of the US astronauts, put together, had spent in space to that date. Orbiting the earth 48 times, she took photographs of the horizon and the sun, and made astronomical observations. She also achieved the other essential aim of her mission: to prove a woman could survive in space.

She parachuted back to a hero's welcome, including a parade in Red Square, alongside her fellow cosmonaut, Valery Bykovsky. The leader of the Soviet Union, Nikita Khrushchev, presented them both with the country's highest honour, the Order of Lenin. 'The bourgeoisie always claim that women are the weaker sex,' said Khrushchev. 'Now here you can see a typical Soviet woman who in the eyes of the bourgeoisie is weak. Look at what she has shown to America's astronauts. She has shown them who is who!'

In the US magazine *Life*, the writer, former Republican politician and ambassador, Clare Booth Luce, wrote angrily about NASA's failure to win this particular race. Astronauts were symbols of prestige and honour, and 'in entrusting a 26-year-old girl with a cosmonaut mission, the Soviet Union has given its women unmistakable proof that it believes them to possess these same virtues. The flight of Valentina Tereshkova is, consequently, symbolic of the emancipation of the Communist woman. It symbolises to Russian women that they actively share (not passively bask, like American women) in the glory of conquering space.'

Tereshkova yearned to return to space, but this never happened. In 1969, that first pioneering group of women cosmonauts was dissolved, and Tereshkova went on to gain a doctorate in engineering, and to hold a number of prominent political positions. It would be nineteen years before Svetlana Savitskaya, another Soviet cosmonaut, became the second woman in space, in July 1982; Sally Ride became the first US woman in space in June 1983.

Tereshkova is still regarded as a hero in Russia, and her fame lives on far beyond. Not only is there a crater on the moon named after her, but also an asteroid, 1671 Chaika.

Miriam Makeba

Singer, 1932–2008

Miriam Makeba, 1967.

'I'm not a politician; I am a singer. Long ago, they said, "That one, she sings politics." I don't sing politics; I merely sing the truth.'

Miriam Makeba's voice took her everywhere. It prompted friendships with presidents and movie stars, led her to jazz clubs and UN assemblies, into exile from South Africa and fame around the world. She became known as 'Mama Africa' and was granted honorary citizenship by ten countries. One of the first African international superstars, she was also the first African woman to win a Grammy, with music blending jazz, pop, folk and gospel, sung in Zulu, Xhosa, French, Spanish and English, earning her the sobriquet 'the nightingale', and leaving US critics struggling to describe her. She had the clarity of Joan Baez, they said, the authority of Sarah Vaughan, the smokiness of Ella Fitzgerald, and the warmth of Frank Sinatra. In other words, she was indefinable; utterly herself. Makeba spoke out against apartheid in South Africa, and when she died, aged 76, it was just after singing her biggest hit, irresistible dance number 'Pata Pata', at a benefit in Italy for a journalist being pursued by mafia-like criminals. Did anyone ever make better, braver use of their voice?

Makeba was born sixteen years before apartheid was imposed in South Africa, but from her earliest days she experienced racism. Her mother Christina was a nurse, and her father Caswell became a clerk for the Shell corporation; when Makeba was eighteen days old, their house was raided by police. Her mother had been making beer to sell to neighbours, but as Makeba writes in her 1987 memoir, the laws of the era dictated that black South Africans were not 'civilised' enough to drink. Makeba spent her first six months in a jail cell with her mother. '"Once in jail, you have to go back at least three times," my mother tells me. She will repeat this when I am older,' Makeba writes. 'And she will be right. I will be going to jail a lot in my life.'

Makeba's father died when she was five, and as she grew up, she discovered a love of singing, starting in a church choir. The apartheid system began as her schooling ended in the late 1940s, and Makeba was employed as a servant to a succession of white families. After she asked the first family for her pay, her female employer accused her of theft and called the police – it turned out she had used this tactic to fire three previous maids without paying them. At the instruction of the second family, Makeba spent months collecting shells on a beach, only to be accused by the police of loitering to sell sex.

Makeba married a policeman, a short relationship, scarred by domestic abuse, which produced her only child, her daughter Bongi. Her singing career began in earnest with The Manhattan Brothers, one of South Africa's most popular bands, followed by her all-female group The Skylarks, and while Makeba experienced her first wave of success, her life was as damaged by racism as ever. Black South Africans were not permitted to record songs in English (she broke the colour bar and did so anyway); weren't allowed to own property; her daughter and other black children were educated just enough to become servants; and when she toured the country, she had to travel with cooking utensils, because restaurants wouldn't serve her. The police could – and did – throw Makeba and her bandmates into jail on a whim, and the severity of the discrimination became most painfully clear when she was travelling in a van of black performers, which crashed. The injured group were left in the road by the authorities who arrived at the scene, and when two passersby drove them to the nearest hospital – a white hospital – they were left untreated. One of the men died. 'I have just looked genocide in the face,' Makeba wrote later.

US filmmaker Lionel Rogosin asked her to sing in a documentary he was making about apartheid, *Come Back, Africa*, and she was invited to the US, to appear on TV and take up a residency at the Village Vanguard in New York. Sidney Poitier, Nina Simone, Miles Davis and Elizabeth Taylor attended her gigs, and Marlon Brando became a friend. Her mentor Harry Belafonte declared she was 'easily the most revolutionary new talent to appear in any medium in the last decade' (it was with him that she won a Grammy in 1966, for their album *An Evening with Belafonte/Makeba*).

When Makeba's mother died in 1960, she tried to return home, but at the South African consulate her passport was stamped 'invalid'. She was officially in exile. And rather than silencing her, as was perhaps hoped, she spoke out more determinedly. In 1963, she appeared before the United Nations Special Committee on Apartheid. 'I appeal to the UN to use its influence to open the doors of all prisons and concentration camps in South Africa, where thousands of our people – men, women and children – are now in jail,' she said. With this, she became, 'a symbol of my repressed people,' she writes. And it became illegal, in South Africa, to sell her music.

Makeba had five marriages, including two years with trumpeter Hugh Masekela, and ten with radical activist Stokely Carmichael. This relationship began in the late 1960s, and as Carmichael began working with the Black Panthers, Makeba found their every move shadowed by the FBI; her gigs and recording work immediately dried up. She and Carmichael moved to Guinea, where she found herself in double exile, barred from her own country, and increasingly unwelcome in western countries.

She lived through divorces, cancer, a coup in Guinea, the death of her grandson Themba, and the mental illness and death of her daughter Bongi, who, she believed, lost her sanity due to exile.

Her own exile finally ended in 1990, four months after Nelson Mandela's release from prison, and she was greeted with great love in South Africa. She worked with Mandela's wife, Graça Machel, to help children suffering with HIV/AIDS, child soldiers and those with disabilities. 'Her hauning melodies gave voice to the pain of exile and dislocation which she felt for 31 long years,' Mandela said when she died. 'She was a mother to our struggle'.

Sophia Duleep Singh

Suffragette, 1876–1948

Sophia Duleep Singh.

The art galleries at Hampton Court Palace were closed, subject to an unspecified threat from the suffragettes. This was 1913, the height of the militant movement, when the campaign for women's votes included arson, window smashing and iconoclasm – paintings slashed or vandalised.

But outside Hampton Court Palace, the area where she lived in a grace and favour apartment, Sophia Duleep Singh was selling copies of the newspaper *The Suffragette*. Public anger towards the campaigners was growing, but she would not be silenced. Photographs show her in a fur coat, her bag bearing a 'Votes for Women' sash, beside a sandwich board reading 'The Suffragette Revolution!'

The struggle for votes for women then stretched back more than a century in Britain. In 1792, Mary Wollstonecraft had made the case for women's right to political representation in *A Vindication of the Rights of Woman*, and the first petition for the women's vote was presented to the House of Commons in 1832. Forty years later, Emmeline Pankhurst, aged fourteen, attended her very first women's suffrage meeting, and when she was in her mid-forties, in 1903, she co-founded the Women's Social and Political Union (WSPU).

The non-militant movement, known as suffragists, led by Millicent Garrett Fawcett, had been campaigning carefully and determinedly for years, but with the advent of Pankhurst's suffragettes (a diminutive and pejorative coined by *The Daily Mail* newspaper, which the women embraced) the next decade was explosive. Women chained themselves to the Prime Minister's railings; unveiled a banner on a steam launch on the Thames; and took to the skies in a balloon, scattering suffragette leaflets.

Around 1,000 suffragettes were imprisoned in Britain over the course of a decade, and in 1909, artist Marion Wallace Dunlop went on hunger strike, demanding recognition as a political prisoner. Other women followed her lead and the authorities responded with forcible feeding: a tube forced into a woman's mouth, nose, or rectum. In June 1913, Emily Wilding Davison was martyred for the movement, stepping on to the racecourse at the Epsom Derby into the path of the king's horse Anmer, a suffragette banner rolled up in her hand, another pinned around her waist. She died in hospital four days later, and suffragettes processed through London, dressed in white, to mark her funeral.

Sophia Duleep Singh joined the WSPU in 1908, after meeting Una Dugdale, a passionate member, who became the first woman in England to drop the word 'obey' from her wedding vows. As Anita Anand writes in her essential 2015 biography of Singh, her activities began, gently enough, with fundraising and bake sales, but in 1909 she became part of the tax resistance movement – women who refused to pay taxes on the basis that there should be no taxation without political representation. On 18 November 1910, Singh was in the vanguard of nine women, including Emmeline Pankhurst, who led a march on parliament, after the latest bill to secure the women's vote had been deprived the time needed to pass. When they reached parliament, the group found themselves pressed up against the gates, unable to enter. Not far away, more suffragettes were massing, and Singh watched helplessly as they were brutalised and molested by police and the crowds, in what became known as Black Friday.

This didn't dent Singh's commitment. In 1911, she joined the suffragette action to subvert the census, one of thousands of women who stayed out on the night of the count, because 'if women don't count, neither should they be counted'. That same year, Singh staged her most audacious protest, hurling herself at Prime Minister Herbert Asquith's car, pulling a banner from her fur muff reading 'Give women the vote!'

This presented a problem for the authorities. Singh was the goddaughter of Queen Victoria, and the granddaughter of Ranjit Singh, the so-called Lion of the Punjab, founder and ruler of the Sikh Empire in India. A decade after Ranjit Singh's death, his son Duleep Singh, aged eleven, had been forced to sign over his kingdom to the British, who took control of the territory and proceeded to expel him. He was brought to Britain, where Queen Victoria treated him as an exotic pet, and he was given an annual income by the India Office.

Duleep Singh married Bamba Müller, the child of a German merchant and an Abyssinian slave, and they had seven children, six of whom survived infancy. Sophia Duleep Singh was the second youngest.

A rift opened in her parents' marriage while Singh was a child; her father was increasingly unfaithful and his anger at the British deepened. Her mother was lost to a serious depression and drank dangerously, before dying of renal failure when Singh was eleven. Duleep Singh was in Russia, and the care of his children was left to the palace and the government.

Singh became a debutante, moving into a house opposite Hampton Court Palace, her life a round of parties, banquets, shopping and dog shows. But trips to India in her twenties and thirties changed everything. The campaign against British colonial rule awoke Singh's political consciousness, and on returning to Britain she wrote in her diary of her loathing for the English and desire for India to awake and free itself.

Her dog show days were over. Singh campaigned in support of the lascars, merchant seamen from India and China who were recruited by the British to transport cargo and often exploited, beaten, or left to starve. She became a suffragette, and when Emmeline Pankhurst called for the suspension of campaigning at the start of the First World War, she worked at one of the British hospitals where Indian soldiers were being cared for.

In 1918, women over 30 who owned property won the right to vote in the UK; in 1928, women secured voting rights on the same terms as men. The suffrage campaign was over, but Singh's commitment to women's rights was lifelong. In *Who's Who*, under interests, she simply wrote, 'The Advancement of Women'.

Sophie Scholl
Anti-Nazi activist, 1921–1943

Sophie Scholl, member of the resistance group the White Rose, c. 1941.

> *'One should do only what is true and good and take it for granted that others will do the same'*

What courage did it take to speak out against the Nazis as a German citizen in the early 1940s? Sophie Scholl recognised the dangers. In October 1942, aged 21, she wrote to her boyfriend, Fritz Hartnagel, a career soldier serving on the Stalingrad front, that her life was plagued with insecurity. 'Every word, before it's uttered, has to be considered from all sides to see if the slightest shimmer of ambiguity exists. Trust in other people has to give way to suspicion and watchfulness. Oh, it's exhausting and discouraging'.

Her paranoia must have been bolstered by her father's recent prison sentence. Robert Scholl had just been released after two months of a four month term, betrayed to the Gestapo by his secretary, who heard him remark that Hitler was a 'scourge of humanity'. It wasn't the family's first run-in with the notorious secret police. In 1937, when Sophie was sixteen, she and her siblings Hans, Inge and Werner had all been arrested as part of a crackdown on illegal youth activity (Hans had previously been a member of an underground youth group, and the others were part of a secret reading group). Sophie was released that day, Inge and

Werner were held for a week, and Hans for a month. It was a clear warning.

But by the time Sophie Scholl wrote that letter to her boyfriend, she was a dedicated member of the White Rose, a group that had decided spiritual resistance to the Nazis was not nearly enough. Scholl's involvement began when she went to study biology and philosophy at the University of Munich, just before her 21st birthday. Her older brother Hans was a medical student there, and one day she went to his room, carrying a leaflet she'd found under a desk at a lecture. Its contents were shocking and thrilling. It was the responsibility of everyone, the leaflet proclaimed, 'to arm himself as best he can to work against the scourge of humanity, against fascism and every other form of the absolute state.' It then quoted the writer Friedrich Schiller.

Hans wasn't home, and Sophie began leafing through a volume of Schiller on his shelf. As Annette Dumbach and Jud Newborn recount in *Sophie Scholl and the White Rose*, the book fell open to a page where the quoted passage was underlined. When Sophie confronted Hans, he denied being involved with the White Rose, but she knew he was lying. She decided to join them.

The group comprised three other medical students alongside Hans – Alexander Schmorell, Willi Graf and Christoph Probst. Later, it also included a professor called Kurt Huber. Sophie Scholl helped distribute the group's leaflets, a process which became increasingly ambitious and dangerous. By the time of their fifth leaflet, 'A Call to All Germans', the plan was for members of the group to travel to one city and send leaflets to individual addresses in another. They would board a train, leave the suitcase in one carriage and sit in another carriage as far away as possible (all trains were now controlled by the Gestapo, who prowled them for deserters, fugitives and smugglers). The suitcase would be retrieved at their destination, where they took to the streets alone, often at night, searching for postboxes. Sophie Scholl's trip took her to Stuttgart, where she posted 800 leaflets.

This caught the Gestapo's attention. Suddenly, it seemed, there was a resistance network operating across the country. The White Rose officially posed a threat to the regime, and the hunt for them was on.

In early adolescence, the Scholl siblings had at first accepted Hitler's ascendance, although their father despised him from the start. Robert Scholl was mayor of a number of small towns in south-west Germany, before the family settled in Ulm in 1932, where he began working as a tax and business consultant. Sophie Scholl joined the female wing of the Hitler Youth and Hans Scholl was a leading figure in the city's male wing, chosen to carry the group's banner at the Nuremberg Party Rally of 1936. But he soon chafed at the authoritarianism. He and the other Scholl children began asking their father about the concentration camps – could Hitler possibly be aware of them? Robert Scholl assured them he was.

As the Gestapo searched for the White Rose, the group prepared their sixth leaflet. On 18 February 1943 Sophie and Hans Scholl headed to the University of Munich, carrying a suitcase. Lectures were underway, the corridors clear, as they began distributing piles of leaflets outside each hall. Then they climbed the stairs, scattering the last leaflets into the atrium. A building custodian shouted that they were under arrest and they were led to the University Rector's office, where the Gestapo chief Robert Mohr was summoned.

During the interrogation, Mohr tried to convince Sophie to betray her brother, to say she didn't share his views and supported Hitler. She refused. 'You're wrong,' she said. 'I would do it all over again.'

A few days later, Hans and Sophie Scholl, along with Christoph Probst, were tried for aiding and abetting the enemy and committing acts of high treason (Probst had been identified through his handwriting – Hans was carrying a handwritten draft of another leaflet when he was arrested). During the brief trial, Sophie interrupted notorious Nazi judge Roland Freisler more than once. 'What we said and wrote are what many people are thinking,' she said. 'They just don't dare say it out loud!' That day, the three were condemned to death and beheaded by guillotine.

All six members of the White Rose were executed that year – and later, too, Hans Conrad Leipelt, who had helped distribute their leaflets. But their words lived on. The Allied forces printed thousands of their leaflets, dropping them from planes all over Germany.

Jan Morris

Writer, 1926–2020

Jan Morris, pictured at her home near the village of
Llanystumdwy in Gwynedd, Wales.

> *'When in life I have succeeded in something, it is generally because I have been ashamed to fail'*

In 1953, Jan Morris went up a mountain and came down a sensation. A journalist for *The Times*, writing under her birth name, James Morris, she had been sent to cover the latest mission to conquer Mount Everest; she was chosen, she wrote later, because of her physical fitness relative to her boozy Fleet Street colleagues. 'The competition would be intense and very likely violent,' she wrote in her 1974 memoir *Conundrum*, 'communications were primitive to a degree, and the only way to do the job was to climb fairly high up the mountain myself and periodically, to put a complex operation simply, run down it again with the news'.

She climbed 22,000 feet in all, and on hearing the summit had been reached, sent a coded message to *The Times* through an Indian Army radio transmitter: 'Snow conditions bad. Stop. Advanced base abandoned yesterday. Stop. Awaiting improvement. Stop. All well.' Her colleagues rushed out the news on the day of Queen Elizabeth II's coronation. Morris had 'scooped the world', she wrote later; she was now the most famous newspaper journalist in the UK. In her 1989 memoir, *Pleasures of a Tangled Life*, she wrote that, 'the moment when, turning on the radio in my tent somewhere in the Sola Khumbu country, I learnt that my message had reached London safely, was a moment that changed my life. The world seemed to open its doors for me. Dinners and banquets beckoned me. I was interviewed in other newspapers, writing engagements multiplied, my first book was commissioned and in a flash I was awarded a fellowship in the United States'.

She travelled across the US for a year for that first book, *Coast to Coast* (1956), and became known as a travel writer, although she preferred to be called simply a writer. Before her trip to Mount Everest, she had already travelled extensively, after joining the army, aged seventeen, in the final throes of the Second World War. Her time as a teenage intelligence officer for the 9th Queen's Royal Lancers took her to Egypt, Austria and Palestine, as well as to Venice, the city that would become the eponymous subject of perhaps her most famous book. After leaving the army she met her wife Elizabeth, and the couple married in Cairo in 1949, where Morris was working for the Arab News Agency. As her career progressed post-Everest, she became a foreign correspondent for the *Manchester Guardian*, scooping the world again with her coverage of the Suez Crisis.

Morris would travel across other boundaries too. In the first paragraphs of *Conundrum* she described the moment she first realised she had been born in the wrong body, sitting beneath her mother's piano, aged three or four. She had no idea where the thought had come from, but the conviction persisted from then on that she was, 'feminine by gender but male by sex, and I could achieve completeness only when the one was adjusted to the other'.

She and Elizabeth had five children together, including a daughter who died at a few months' old, and in 1961 Morris gave up her job as a journalist to write books. She was a great success, her writing lauded and loved, but suffered periods of depression. Her wife was well aware of her feelings. 'I hid nothing of my dilemma from Elizabeth,' she wrote in *Conundrum*, 'explaining it to her as I had never explained it before: I told her that through each year my every instinct seemed to become more feminine, my entombment within the male physique more terrible to me.' By her mid-thirties she felt repugnant, and a few years later, in 1964, she began taking hormones.

In 1972, Morris went to a specialist doctor in Casablanca for surgery. She and Elizabeth divorced after her transition, but remained together, and renewed their union with a civil partnership in 2008. They plan to be buried together, beneath a headstone with the inscription: 'Here lie two friends, at the end of one life.'

Morris had started *Pax Britannica*, her trilogy on the rise and fall of the British Empire, before her transition; speaking to the *Paris Review*, she described the idea like this: 'Supposing in the last years of the Roman Empire one young centurion, old enough to remember the imperial impulses and the imperial splendour, but recognising that it was passing, sat down and wrote a large book about his sensations at that moment. Wouldn't that be interesting?' The concern that transition might affect her writing talent proved unfounded, of course, as did worries about her long-term health. In a 1974 interview concerning her transition, Morris said, 'nobody so far has done this and lived to a ripe old age, you know'. But she did, living to the age of 94.

Activist Christine Burns has written that Morris's transition never diminished her 'ability to pursue her career, which is the most valuable reassurance that anyone can give to a young trans person standing on the brink of following the same path to personal congruity'. In a career spanning more than 40 books, considered one of the greatest of all post-war British authors, she remained intrepid to the last.

Junko Tabei

Mountaineer, 1939–2016

Junko Tabei, c. 1975.

*'Climbing the mountain
is its own reward'*

In 1975, Junko Tabei became the first woman to reach the summit of Mount Everest. In doing so, she defied the men who refused to climb with her when she first took up mountaineering; defied those who suggested she should stay at home to look after her daughter; and braved perils including a near-fatal avalanche, and a journey along an icy ridge where a single misstep would have meant falling thousands of metres. 'I can't understand why men make all this fuss about Everest,' she said after reaching the summit. 'It's only a mountain.'

The US mountaineer Fanny Bullock Workman had been photographed on the Siachen Glacier in the Himalayas 63 years earlier, one of the least explored, least accessible places in the world. In the picture her face is obscured by a newspaper, its front page presented carefully to display the headline: 'Votes for Women'. The symbolism is clear. Women were barred from voting in almost every country at the time, and the implicit and often explicit justification was that they were weaker than men, intellectually and physically.

Workman's image punctured the idea that women and weakness are synonymous, the biological determinism used to bar women from public life. And Tabei's achievement six decades later was a majestic riposte to such arguments, and to all the people who had told her that no woman would ever conquer the mountain.

Born in 1939, in a small town in northern Japan, Tabei was the fifth daughter in a family of seven children. A sickly child, with weak lungs, she first climbed two peaks – Mount Asahi and Mount Chausu – with classmates, aged ten. After studying English Literature at Showa Women's University, she joined a number of climbing clubs in the early 1960s, telling the writer Robert Horn, years later, 'some of the men wouldn't climb with me, but a few older ones were more supportive. Some thought I was there to meet men, but I was only interested in climbing'.

She married mountaineer Masanobu Tabei and in 1969 set up Japan's first climbing club for women. In 1970, the group decided to tackle the Himalayan mountain Annapurna III and on succeeding, were keen to try Everest; with expeditions strictly limited at the time, they had to wait until 1975 to make their attempt. In the meantime, they prepared, seeking the necessary sponsorship, although most companies' reaction, Tabei has said, 'was that for women, it's impossible to climb Mount Everest'. The group of fifteen women included teachers, a computer programmer and a youth counsellor, and they saved money where possible by making waterproof pouches out of recycled car seat covers and accepting unused packets of jam from their students.

Tabei was told she should stay at home to look after her young daughter, but, 'there was never a question in my mind that I wanted to climb that mountain, no matter what other people said'. As the group started their attempt, newspaper articles mocked them. 'They would use the picture of us applying a lip balm and say "even in the mountain, they don't skip wearing the make up",' Tabei said later. 'For a lot of people, it was a joke. They didn't think we could make it.'

The most perilous moment came on 4 May 1975, when the group reached 21,326 feet above sea level, and their camp was hit by an avalanche. Just before Tabei passed out, an image of her daughter flashed through her mind, and she was saved by the team's Sherpas, who pulled her out by her ankles from underneath the snow and the four teammates who had fallen on top of her. Immediately afterwards, she couldn't walk. But two days later, with a wrenched lower back and legs, she rose to her feet, and assumed her place as the group's leader, climbing and sometimes crawling towards the summit.

Less than 100 metres from the peak, she was faced with an icy ridge, fourteen or fifteen metres long – if she fell in one direction she would plummet 5,000 metres into China; if she fell the other, it was a 6,400 metre fall into Nepal. 'I had never felt that tense in my entire life,' she told The Japan Times. But she crawled carefully along the ridge, and made it to the top at 12.35pm on 16 May 1975. She felt relief, she has said, rather than elation.

In 1992, Tabei became the first woman in the world to climb the highest mountain on each of the seven continents. She undertook graduate studies at Kyushu University, researching the problem of the rubbish left on Mount Everest, and spoke out strongly for environmental protection of the mountain. 'When I reached the summit, rather than simply feeling the joy of conquering the mountain, I felt that at last I did not have to take another single step,' Tabei once said. Her achievement was an enormous step for all women.

Nora Ephron

Writer and director, 1941–2012

Nora Ephron in Los Angeles, California, 1978.

> *'Above all, be the heroine of your life, not the victim'*

The child of two screenwriters and the oldest of four writer sisters, Nora Ephron grew up in Beverly Hills with her mother's words – 'Everything is copy' – echoing around her. She quickly came to realise the power of moulding life's horrors and humiliations into something witty and reassuring. 'When you slip on a banana peel, people laugh at you; but when you tell people you slipped on a banana peel, it's your laugh,' she once wrote. 'So you become the hero rather than the victim of the joke.'

Ephron's life had been played for laughs since before she could speak. Her earliest moments were immortalised on Broadway when she was two, in her parents' play *Three's a Family*; in 1963, the letters she wrote to her parents while studying at Wellesley became the basis for the film *Take Her, She's Mine* starring James Stewart and Sandra Dee. Her parents were both lapsing into alcoholism during her late adolescence, but it is difficult to tell if Ephron felt the bite of this. (Her approach to all life events was to make them into an excellent story, ideally with an upbeat ending.)

At Wellesley, as she explained in a commencement address there in 1996, 'we weren't meant to have futures; we were meant to marry them . . . If you wanted to be an architect, you married an architect.' Her ambition, instead, was to move to New York and become Dorothy Parker, which made sense in terms of her wit, but not her temperament (she has been called Pollyannaish, not a quality associated with Parker, who once wrote a verse called 'Resumé', listing ways to kill oneself).

In her early twenties, Ephron was a reporter for the *New York Post*. Then she wrote an essay about her breasts, became a writer and was soon one of the most prominent and honest chroniclers of the 1970s women's movement. She wrote about the gap between true sexual liberation and women's masochistic sexual fantasies ('I doubt that it will ever be possible for the women of my generation to escape from our own particular slave mentality'); the challenges of solidarity ('like all things about liberation, sisterhood is difficult'); Betty Friedan's 'thoroughly irrational hatred' of Gloria Steinem; and her reaction to the news that a group of women were meeting up to observe their cervixes with a speculum ('it is hard not to long for the days when an evening with the girls meant bridge').

She married writer Dan Greenburg in her mid-twenties, divorced, and then married journalist Carl Bernstein. He and fellow reporter Bob Woodward had uncovered the Watergate scandal, and wrote the book *All the President's Men*, which then became a film. Ephron rewrote the original screenplay, and although her version was never used, this led to a new career. She would go on to be Academy Award nominated for three screenplays: *Silkwood*, *Sleepless in Seattle* and *When Harry Met Sally*.

The breakdown of her marriage to Bernstein also led her to become a novelist. She turned the tumult and heartbreak into the funny, excoriating roman à clef *Heartburn*, and Bernstein threatened to sue her. (The novel's most famous line concerns the cheating husband who, Ephron writes, was 'capable of having sex with a Venetian blind'.)

For the men who ran Hollywood, she realised, 'A movie about a woman's cure for cancer is less interesting than a movie about a man with a hangnail'. So she decided to become a director, to tell the stories she wanted to tell, including the reassuring and romantic fables *You've Got Mail* and *Julie and Julia*. In a *New Yorker* magazine profile by Ariel Levy in 2009, Ephron spoke about the necessity of getting on with the creative act. 'Nobody really has an easy time getting a movie made,' she said. 'And furthermore I can't stand people complaining . . . Those *endless* women-in-film panels. It's, like, just do it! Just *do* it. Write something else if this one didn't get made. It's my ongoing argument with a whole part of the women's movement.'

Panels on Women in Film were one of the things she cited in her late essay on the subject 'What I Won't Miss' (its counterpart, 'What I Will Miss', ended 'Taking a bath / Coming over the bridge to Manhattan / Pie'). But Ephron's impatience with that strain of women's activism didn't denote a general disdain for feminism. In her speech to those graduating students in 1996, she ended by advising them to 'find some way to break the rules and make a little trouble out there. And I also hope that you will choose to make some of that trouble on behalf of women.' She mentored young women writers; when Ephron died, Lena Dunham wrote that 'the opportunity to be friends with Nora in the last year of her life informs the entirety of mine'.

In her final years, she was faced with something she couldn't turn into comedy, a blood disorder called myelodysplastic syndrome. She knew telling people would prompt pity, and could also affect her ability to secure funding and insurance for her movies. So she told only a small circle of friends and relatives, including her third husband, the writer Nick Pileggi, to whom she was married for the best part of three decades (her own happy, romantic ending, worthy of the montage of long-time couples in *When Harry Met Sally*).

Meryl Streep played Ephron's alter ego in the film of *Heartburn*, was directed by her in *Julie and Julia*, and spoke at her funeral. 'You could call on her for anything: doctors, restaurants, recipes, speeches, or just a few jokes, and we all did it constantly. She was an expert in all the departments of living well.' What could be better than that?

Audre Lorde

Writer, 1934–1992

Audre Lorde, 1983.

> *'When we speak we are afraid our words will not be heard nor welcomed. But when we are silent, we are still afraid. So it is better to speak'*

Audre Lorde's life was dedicated to making the unseen seen. She was a woman. She was black. She was a lesbian. She was a socialist, a poet, a mother, an activist and a teacher, and for the last decade and a half of her life she was a person living with cancer. As her friend and fellow poet Jackie Kay once wrote, 'Lorde was Whitman-like in her refusal to be confined to single categories. She was large. She contained multitudes'. She knew if you denied one part of yourself the whole edifice was jeopardised.

Lorde's legacy and influence has grown since her death in 1992. During that period, the theory of intersectionality has become perhaps the dominant strand in western feminist thought – a theory first coined in those terms by the US academic Kimberlé Crenshaw in 1989. This suggests that in order to understand discrimination, prejudice and possible remedies, we have to understand how people's identities intersect, and to honour those identities.

These are ideas Lorde discussed throughout her career. In her essay 'There is no Hierarchy of Oppressions', she wrote about sexism, heterosexism and racism, and how these arose from the same source – a belief in the inherent superiority of one mode of being above all others, and thereby its right to dominance. 'I cannot afford to choose between the fronts upon which I must battle these forces of discrimination, wherever they appear to destroy me,' she wrote. 'And when they appear to destroy me, it will not be long before they appear to destroy you.'

Born in New York in 1934, Lorde was the third daughter of an immigrant family, her father from Barbados, her mother from Grenada; she didn't speak until she was four and her short-sightedness made her legally blind. She describes these years in *Zami: A New Spelling of My Name*, which blends autobiography and fiction. As such, it's difficult to know which individual details of the book are straightforwardly true, but it conjures the texture of the times. As a small girl, she writes, she would shrink 'from a particular sound, a hoarsely sharp, guttural rasp, because it often meant a nasty glob of grey spittle upon my coat or shoe an instant later'. Her mother would wipe this off with newspaper and fuss about low-class people spitting into the wind. It was years before Lorde realised she had been their target.

The family moved from Harlem to an apartment in a 'changing' neighbourhood and two weeks later their land-lord hanged himself in the basement. '*The Daily News* reported that the suicide was caused by his despondency over the fact that he finally had to rent to Negroes,' writes Lorde. On her graduation from the eighth grade, the family went to Washington D.C., and stopped by a soda fountain for an ice cream. The five of them sat at the counter and the waitress said they could not eat there. 'My parents wouldn't speak of this injustice,' writes Lorde, 'not because they had contributed to it, but because they felt they should have anticipated and avoided it. This made me even angrier. My fury was not going to be acknowledged by a like fury.'

Lorde also charts the excitement of being a young lesbian in the 1950s, frequenting New York's gay bars and having her first sexual encounters, her writing in *Zami* encompassing joy as well as pain. In her 1978 essay 'The Uses of the Erotic', she writes about how the erotic has been used against women, and confused with pornography, which 'represents the suppression of true feeling'. Lorde defines the erotic, instead, as 'an internal sense of satisfaction to which, once we have experienced it, we know we can aspire' – a benchmark for excellence and connection. Women 'have been raised to fear the "yes" within ourselves,' she writes.

Lorde was active in the civil rights movement and feminism, and campaigned for gay and lesbian rights – when discrimination occurred within these movements, she took the hard path and spoke about it. In the 1960s she married an attorney, Edwin Rollins, and had two children, Elizabeth and Jonathan; in 1968, she published her first book of poetry; and in 1970 she divorced, and began a decades long relationship with Frances Clayton, a professor of psychology. She published many volumes of poetry, gave hundreds of speeches, and became one of the co-founders of Kitchen Table, the first publishing house in the US for women of colour. The work continued after she was diagnosed with breast cancer, then liver cancer. In her book *A Burst of Light*, a journal of these years, she wrote that she considered the time she spent looking after her body each day, 'part of my political work. It is possible to have some conscious input into our physical processes – not expecting the impossible, but allowing for the unexpected – a kind of training in self-love and physical resistance.'

By being open about all her identities, Lorde changed the lives of others. In *A Burst of Light* she writes about Harlem Renaissance poet Angelina Weld Grimké, who was black and thought to be a lesbian. As a young lesbian herself, Lorde wrote that she had often thought of Grimké dying alone in New York in 1958, 'and I think of what it could have meant in terms of sisterhood and survival for each one of us to have known of the other's existence: for me to have had her words and her wisdom, and for her to have known I needed them!' When Jackie Kay first read Lorde's book of poetry, *The Black Unicorn*, in Brixton, London, in 1981, 'it was like finding a friend,' she once wrote. 'Her work told me I was not alone.'

Lucille Ball

Comedian, 1911–1989

Lucille Ball as Lucy Ricardo in the popular TV series
I Love Lucy, c. 1955.

> *'I'm not funny.*
> *What I am is brave.'*

Was improving the representation of women upper-most in Lucille Ball's mind when *I Love Lucy* began in 1951? It seems unlikely. Ball was approaching 40, and after two decades of work, starting as a model in New York, she was still intent on making her name. Since arriving in Hollywood in her early twenties, there had been stints as a contract player for RKO and MGM, appearances in comedies opposite the Marx Brothers and Gene Kelly, dramatic roles opposite Katharine Hepburn and Ginger Rogers, and in her thirties she had risen to the iffy status of queen of the B movies. There were forays into musical comedy, work on stage, a successful move into radio acting, but still, she was searching. 'I had a driving, consuming ambition to succeed in show business,' she wrote in her autobiography *Love, Lucy*, in 1964, 'but I had no idea where my real talents lay. I was dying to be told, to be shown. Way down deep underneath those brassy showgirl trappings was Lucy, and there she stayed, strangulated, for years'.

Television was in its infancy, and while many movie stars disdained it, she saw it as a chance to try something new – ideally alongside her husband, Desi Arnaz. She had married

Arnaz, a Cuban-born bandleader, six years her junior, in 1940, and the union was rocky. The pair spent long periods apart when Arnaz was out on the road; Ball even started divorce proceedings in 1944. They reconciled, but for all their desire to work together, TV and movie bosses couldn't conceive of them as a couple on screen. The public wanted to see all-American husband and wife teams, they supposed. Arnaz was just too Cuban.

The pair decided to start a production company called Desilu, and went on tour with a vaudeville act. 'Desi sang and played the bongo drums,' wrote Ball, while she, 'kept trying to butt into his nightclub act. I also did a baggy-pants routine with a cello loaded with a stool, a plunger, flowers, and other props, and flipped and barked like a seal.'

The show was a hit, word reached TV producers, and they were given the chance to make a series, appearing as a married couple. The show built on the couple's vaudeville act, with Arnaz as a band leader and Ball as his wife, who stayed at home but dreamed of breaking into show business. It was an immediate hit, reaching number one in its first season, and retaining that position for four of its six series.

Arguments persist over whether *I Love Lucy* was in any sense a feminist show – there were, apparently, four occasions when Arnaz put Ball over his knee on screen and spanked her, which suggests not. His character, Ricky Ricardo, was a chauvinist; her character, Lucy Ricardo, was a housewife. But Lucy was a character who wanted much more, and although her schemes failed, her ambition never waned. In a decade when many women felt stifled in the home, pushed out of the workplace they had entered during the war, Lucy was a warm, hopeful everywoman, who represented a burning desire for excitement, adventure and a self-actualisation which would be explored in more intellectual form in Betty Friedan's feminist classic *The Feminine Mystique*, in 1963.

Today there are still weary, ridiculous disputes about whether women can be funny – but in the 1950s, Lucille Ball showed, beyond doubt, that a woman could be hilarious and that slapstick, screwball brilliance could make her the undisputed star of the biggest TV series of the era. She broke boundaries beyond that. There was the depiction of a mixed race marriage on screen; the sight of a woman becoming a bona fide star in her forties; and, perhaps most pioneering, the appearance of a pregnant woman on screen. Ball was four months pregnant with her daughter Lucie when she signed the deal for the first series, and this was kept hidden from the audience. But as the second series approached, and Ball learned she was pregnant with Desi Jr, at 40, there were conversations with the producers about whether the series could go ahead. Up to this point, an obviously pregnant woman had never appeared on TV – it was thought to be in bad taste. A priest, minister and rabbi were brought in to adjudicate on the seven episodes concerning her pregnancy, and all agreed they were fine. The network allowed them to go ahead, so long as they used the word 'expecting' rather than 'pregnant', and the birth of little Ricky became one of the TV hits of the century.

The couple had complete ownership of the show from its inception, and presided over the thriving Desilu production company, but their marriage became turbulent again, and the sixth season of *I Love Lucy* was their last. They divorced, and Ball bought Arnaz out of Desilu, and became the first woman to run a major production company.

She went on to star in other successful series, starting with *The Lucy Show*.

In 1967 Ball sold Desilu, and she enjoyed a 28 year marriage to the comedian Gary Morton before her death in 1989. She set out, like her character, to make her name, and in the process – perhaps inadvertently – she improved the representation of women.

Jayaben Desai

Strike leader, 1933–2010

Jayaben Desai as Treasurer of the Grunwick Strike Committee,
picketing in August 1977.

> *'We must not give up.*
> *Would Gandhi give up?*
> *Never!'*

'I want my freedom,' said Jayaben Desai, as she walked out of the Grunwick film processing plant in north London, one dripping hot day in August 1976. Hers wasn't an idle demand. Over the next two years, Desai led a strike over pay and conditions that challenged all the stereotypes of migrant women as subservient and docile. She and her fellow strikers were defined by their determination, persistence, courage and wit, this last quality clear in another of her proclamations to Malcolm Alden, the Grunwick manager, as she downed tools. 'What you are running here is not a factory, it is a zoo. But in a zoo there are many types of animals. Some are monkeys who dance on your fingertips, others are lions who can bite your head off. We are those lions, Mr Manager.'

Desai had campaigned for Indian independence in her youth, after being born in Gujarat, and had come to Britain with her husband Suryakant after a decade living in what is now Tanzania. They were part of a wave of Asian migration prompted by the 'Africanisation' policies sweeping across some newly-independent East African countries. (Most famously, in August 1972, Idi Amin ordered the expulsion from Uganda of all Asian people who were not Ugandan citizens.) But they didn't receive the welcome they might have hoped for as British citizens, with British passports. After a relatively comfortable life in Tanzania, Suryakant took work in the UK as an unskilled labourer, while his wife's first job was as a sewing machinist in a Harlesden sweatshop.

On walking out of the Grunwick plant, Desai and her fellow workers immediately joined the union APEX, and began campaigning for the right to organise. Trade union history in the UK was predominantly white and male to this point, although one of the most significant strikes of the previous decade had been the walkout of women workers at the Ford plant in Dagenham in June 1968, 187 sewing machinists arguing for their right to be paid at the same rates as male workers. That action helped prompt the Equal Pay Act of 1970, which stated that men and women in the UK should receive equal pay for equal work.

At Grunwick there were soon thousands of trade union members protesting on behalf of the women; on one occasion, 20,000 people stood outside the gates of the plant. Mrs Desai, as she was always known, travelled the country, to drum up support, and the trade unionist Jack Dromey remembered her telling a packed meeting of strikers, 'we must not give up. Would Gandhi give up? Never!'

The main business of the plant was developing film – this was where people sent their holiday snaps in the days before digital cameras – and when the local postmen decided to support the strike, and stopped mail from being delivered to the plant, success seemed imminent. (The postal workers faced serious repercussions, including the threat of dismissal, but as their chairman Colin Maloney remarked, 'You don't say 'no' to Mrs Desai'.) A court of inquiry was set up to try to resolve the dispute, and concluded the workers should be reinstated and allowed to join a union. But the Grunwick boss George Ward refused to accept this, and he was supported by Margaret Thatcher who, as leader of the opposition, was gathering strength. Ward was also backed by the majority of the British press, who called Desai and her fellow workers, 'strikers in saris'. After two years, with union support for the strike slipping away, the action was called off. The fight was over.

Desai went on to teach an Asian dressmaking class at Harrow College, and continued to support political and industrial causes. Although the demands of the Grunwick strike were not met, and there is continued debate over its legacy, she and the other strikers changed the perception of women in general, and of migrant women in particular. At their last meeting, she summed up what had been achieved: 'We have shown that workers like us, new to these shores, will never accept being treated without dignity or respect'.

Oprah Winfrey

Television icon, b.1954

Oprah Winfrey at the 14th Annual Daytime Emmy Awards, 1987.

> *'I never did consider or call myself a feminist, but I don't think you can really be a woman in this world and not be'*

In the late 1990s, while preparing for the role of Sethe, a former slave, in the film *Beloved*, Oprah Winfrey underwent a re-enactment of the underground railroad, the perilous network of secret routes and safe houses people used to flee slavery in the US in the nineteenth century. She was blindfolded, left in the wilderness, and verbally abused with racial taunts and sexual threats when she finally reached a human contact. 'Out in the woods,' she told one interviewer, 'what hit me was that the physicality was minor compared with the emotional and spiritual devastation when you know your life is owned'.

Winfrey has slave ancestry, and was brought up in a poor household, her first six years spent on a Mississippi farm, raised by her grandmother, who made sure she could read by the age of three, but who beat her regularly. Oprah would grow up to be a maid, her grandmother imagined, her dream being that Winfrey would have white employers who, 'treat you right, treat you nice'.

Instead, Winfrey became a self-made billionaire, often described as the most influential woman in the world. Her life would never be owned. She took charge first of her TV talk show, and then the Oprah Winfrey Network: the aptly-abbreviated OWN.

All this came after a difficult childhood. Aged six, Winfrey moved to live with her mother Vernita in Wisconsin, and aged nine she was raped; there followed years of molestation, and a pregnancy at fourteen. By this time she was living with her father Vernon in Tennessee, and when Winfrey's baby died within a couple of weeks of being born prematurely, he suggested this was her second chance. She agreed.

Winfrey became a local news anchor in her early twenties, before she moved to Chicago in 1983 to host a half-hour morning talk show. It shot up the ratings, was expanded to an hour, renamed *The Oprah Winfrey Show*, and began broadcasting nationally in September 1986. Years later, in documentary series *Makers*, reflecting on the decision to take ownership of the show, Winfrey said she'd been spurred on by a conversation with her bosses, who said her staff didn't need pay rises, because they were just 'girls'. Winfrey had had her own battles over pay inequality – on a show she presented in 1980 her male co-anchor was paid $50,000, while she was paid $22,000. Her thought process was: 'I want to own my own show, and I want to take the risk of owning my own show so that I will be the one to say who gets what pay cheques.'

The talk show ran from 1986 to 2011 and formed the bedrock of a career including her own magazine, a book club credited with transforming the publishing industry and an Oscar nomination for her acting in *The Color Purple*. 'What we did with the platform of The Oprah Winfrey Show was to validate women, to say, "you matter",' she has said. 'You matter if you've been divorced, you matter if you've been abused. You are not your circumstances, you are what is possible for you.'

Winfrey's shows have enabled her to discuss difficult issues. After her talk show ended she said her biggest regret was that she 'wasn't able to move the needle far enough on abuse in this country'. But she certainly made a difference. She first opened up about her own experience of abuse in an emotional moment on her show in 1986, and went on to testify before the Senate Judiciary Committee in 1991; in 1993, with her support, the National Child Protection Act – which created a database of child abusers – was signed into law by Bill Clinton. She also backed the Combating Child Exploitation Act on her show in 2008 (senators received a deluge of emails and calls from viewers), and the final season of *The Oprah Winfrey Show* included a groundbreaking programme in which 200 men opened up about their experiences of being abused in childhood.

She has used her platform to champion racial equality, with one early show in 1987 including a febrile town hall meeting in Forsyth County, Georgia – the town had been entirely white for 75 years, and the scene of racist demonstrations in the weeks preceding Winfrey's arrival. Through her appearances in films including *Beloved*, *The Color Purple*, *The Butler*, and *Selma*, she has explored the history of slavery, racism and the civil rights movement.

She has also been influential regarding gay rights, perhaps most notably when the comedian Ellen DeGeneres came out on *The Oprah Winfrey Show* in 1997. Winfrey then played a therapist on the episode of DeGeneres's sitcom, *Ellen*, in which the title character came out too.

Within a month of the attacks on the World Trade Centre on 11 September 2001, Winfrey presented an episode of her show entitled 'Islam 101', to improve understanding of the Muslim faith. And in the months before the US-led coalition began its war on Iraq in 2003, hers was one of the few mainstream shows that questioned the legitimacy of such action.

In 2011, Winfrey went from running her own show, to running her own channel, with the launch of the Oprah Winfrey Network. 'The real feminism for me,' she has said, 'was about strength of character, believing that you were worthy, that I was worthy and deserved what everyone else deserved, because I was female and black.' Through her life and work, Winfrey has proved to her enormous constituency – including women, African-Americans, the poor, abandoned and abused – that they have value, and should be seen.

Amelia Earhart

Pilot, b.1897, disappeared 1937, declared dead in absentia 1939

Amelia Earhart, 1932.

'The most effective way to do it is to do it'

In May 1928, preparations were well underway for the flight that would make Amelia Earhart's name. She had made a will, listing her debts, and written letters to her mother, father and sister Muriel, in the event of her death. 'I have tried to play for a large stake,' read the letter to Muriel, 'and if I succeed all will be well. If I don't, I shall be happy to pop off in the midst of such an adventure.'

Earhart was attempting to become the first woman to fly the Atlantic, and would be doing so as a passenger, alongside two male pilots. The first Atlantic crossing in a plane had been made solo by Charles Lindbergh the year before, and had inspired a flurry of ill-fated attempts. Susan Butler describes these in *East to the Dawn*, her definitive 1997 biography of Earhart. In the twelve months after Lindbergh's success, 55 people made the attempt, in eighteen planes – eight people succeeded, and fourteen died. Of the five women who had tried, none had been successful, and three had died.

The odds were inauspicious, and led Amy Phipps Guest – a Pittsburgh heiress married to Winston Churchill's cousin – to abandon her own planned crossing. But she had the pilots and equipment in place, and was determined an

American woman should be first. She instructed her lawyer to find the right person.

The hunt led to Earhart, a social worker in Boston, who had been flying since 1920. The pastime had always been deadly. In the year Earhart first flew, notes Butler, fifteen of the pilots hired by the post office had died; of the first 40 pilots hired in this role, 31 died. This didn't deter Earhart. Asked by Guest's emissary if she'd like to fly the Atlantic, she didn't hesitate.

At least two other women were making serious preparations, so the pressure was intense. On 17 June, Earhart decided they must leave, to beat the others – even though lead pilot, Bill Stultz, seemed nervous and inebriated. (During the flight, she would find his alcohol stash, and a year later, Stultz and two passengers died in a plane crash. The autopsy showed he was 'very drunk'.)

Flying through heavy storms, visibility impeded, they made it to Burry Port in Wales. The reaction to their success was extraordinary; job offers and marriage proposals flooded in for Earhart.

She wasn't the only remarkable woman pilot of the era. In *Women Aviators*, Bernard Marck writes of Marie Marvingt, a French woman known as the Fiancée of Danger, who could drive a train and pilot a steamboat, was one of the world's best mountain climbers, and won the women's flying contest, the Femina Cup, in 1911. As a woman, she was denied the chance to join a fighter squadron during the First World War, so she disguised herself as a man and served as a sharpshooter in the trenches.

The Belgian Hélène Dutrieu, known as the Woman Sparrowhawk, was the women's world cycling champion in the late 1890s, before taking up stunt motorcycling, then flying; she won the inaugural Femina Cup in 1910. Bessie Coleman, an African-American pilot, one of thirteen children of sharecropper parents in Texas, was unable to study flying in the US, on account of her race. She became the first African-American woman to hold a pilot's license after studying in France, and was known as Queen Bess on her return to the US, thrilling the crowds in the 1920s with her loop the loops.

Coleman's success, given both racial and gender boundaries, was phenomenal. As every woman flier knew, the sexism alone could be debilitating. In 1926, women were authorised to pilot commercial planes by the International Commission for Air Navigation – but it was advised they shouldn't have passengers on board; and in 1935, male pilots threatened to strike if Helen Richey was allowed to continue as the first woman in the US hired to fly a mail and passenger route. It's not surprising Earhart advised women that if they wanted to 'knock at the door' of aviation, 'it might be well to bring an axe along; you may have to chop your way through'.

After her groundbreaking flight as a passenger, she was determined to prove herself as a pilot, and did so in style. In November 1929 she broke the women's speed record, and in May 1932, she crossed the Atlantic, flying solo – only Lindbergh had achieved this, to date, and she was the first person to have made the crossing twice in a plane. She established a new women's transcontinental record in July of that year, before becoming the first woman to fly nonstop across the US in August. In 1935 she became the first person to fly solo from Honolulu to California. She was now the first person to have flown solo across both the Atlantic and Pacific oceans.

Earhart was particularly passionate about female independence; as a young woman she started a scrapbook called *Activities of Women*, including articles about a woman fire lookout, film producer, and police commissioner. When she married publisher George Putnam in 1931, she wrote him a letter insisting they should both have sexual freedom, and made clear her reluctance about marriage, 'my feeling that I shatter thereby chances in work which means so much to me'. Three years later, she went to work at Purdue University in a new department for the study of women's careers.

Approaching forty, she decided to fly around the world. This had been achieved before, but she would be travelling 27,000 miles, the longest route yet. On 17 March 1937, she and navigator Fred Noonan set off from Oakland, completing 22,000 miles before they went missing en route to a small US-owned island called Howland in the Pacific. No confirmed trace has ever been found, and speculation persists, unburied. Just after completing that first Atlantic flight, Earhart wrote, 'some day women will fly the Atlantic and think little of it because it is an ordinary thing to do'. She opened up the skies to women, and a boundless sense of possibility.

Artemisia Gentileschi

Artist, c.1593–1653

Self-portrait as the Allegory of Painting by
Artemisia Gentileschi, 1638–9, oil on canvas.

> *'As long as I live I will have control over my being. My illustrious lordship, I'll show you what a woman can do'*

In *Self-Portrait as the Allegory of Painting*, Artemisia Gentileschi's right hand holds a paintbrush while her left holds a palette, and she gazes, with complete absorption, at an easel somewhere just beyond the canvas. The image is audacious. Gentileschi, a woman artist, in 1638 or thereabouts, didn't just place herself at the centre of a painting. She depicted herself as the personification of painting.

In her 1971 essay, 'Why Have There Been No Great Women Artists?', Linda Nochlin discusses what has been required, historically, to become established as a painter. It's not just about a spark of genius, she suggests. Institutional and social structures are needed to enable that spark – structures which have typically only supported male artists. Nochlin illustrates this with a memorable example. From the Renaissance until the end of the nineteenth century, it was essential for anyone wishing to paint professionally to engage in prolonged study of nude models. Trouble was, nude models, of either sex, were completely off limits to women artists. Nochlin cites a 1772 group portrait of the Royal Academy in London, by Johan Zoffany, which makes this very clear. The artists have gathered to study two nude male models. 'All the distinguished members are present,' writes Nochlin, 'with but one noteworthy exception – the single female member, the renowned Angelica Kauffmann, who, for propriety's sake, is merely present in effigy, in the form of a portrait hanging on the wall'.

The barriers facing women artists in this era were legion. Yet Gentileschi, working more than a century before that Zoffany portrait, broke through. Her standing as an artist has been the subject of fierce debate over the last century, arguments made more complicated by the misattribution and loss of some of her work, and by the tendency of critics to read her own violent experience as a young woman into her images, in a familiar conflation of biography and art. But the verdict nonetheless seems clear. In her classic work, *Women, Art and Society*, Whitney Chadwick writes that 'Gentileschi is the first woman artist in the history of western art whose historical significance is unquestionable'. And in the 1979 book, *The Obstacle Race*, Germaine Greer writes that 'Artemisia represents the female equivalent of an Old Master. She is the exception to all the rules: she rejected a conventional feminine role for a revolutionary female one'.

How did Gentileschi achieve this? The answer is partly that she was brought up by an artist father, after her mother died when she was twelve. As Nochlin points out, many male artists have had artist fathers (including Holbein, Raphael, Picasso and Giacometti), and Orazio Gentileschi, a follower of Caravaggio, based in Rome, was important to his daughter's progress because he had a workshop, where he introduced her to all the essentials of painting. This provided her with the necessary support and structure which other women lacked. In 1916, Italian critic Roberto Longhi wrote that Gentileschi was the "only woman in Italy who ever knew what was painting, colour, impasto, and other essentials'.

In 1611, still a teenager, Gentileschi was raped by one of her father's associates, an artist called Agostino Tassi. The case was taken to court, and during the course of the trial, not only did Gentileschi face a gynaecological examination, but the judge decided she should be subjected to thumb-screws, a form of torture, to help him ascertain if she was telling the truth. Her testimony remained steadfast. Tassi and his friends, meanwhile, were insisting that she was (in polite terms) a woman of easy virtue. He was eventually convicted and reportedly sentenced to a period of exile from Rome – a sentence he never served. 'The abortive trial had left Artemisia nothing but her talent,' writes Greer. 'It also removed the traditional obstacle to the development of that talent. She could no longer hope to live a life of matronly seclusion: she was notorious and she had no chance but to take advantage of the fact.'

During or not long after the trial, Gentileschi painted perhaps her most famous work, *Judith Slaying Holofernes*. It shows three figures, tightly framed – a man, still alive, and struggling on a bed, held down at the waist by one woman, while another woman nearer the viewer begins cutting off his head with a sword. The women's expressions are calm and determined, and the one bearing the sword has a muscularity that echoes Gentileschi's self-portraits. Blood spurts from the wound, forming rivulets across the bed.

This scene would have been familiar at the time; both Caravaggio and Gentileschi's father had depicted versions of Judith's story. But the intensity and violence of the image have led some critics to suggest it was a revenge painting, and that much of the artist's work – which went on to depict many powerful, determined women – was influenced by her experience of being raped and testifying against the perpetrator in court. While there may be some truth in this, a danger occurs when biographical readings of Gentileschi's work are used to undermine her artistry – a fate that has always bedevilled women artists. A painting such as *Judith Slaying Holofernes* has a clear emotional resonance, but its drama and movement is achieved through its extraordinary composition; its success is based on ingenuity and skill.

When Gentileschi went to work in Florence, she became the first woman member of the Academy of the Arts of Drawing, and her artistic career took her to Venice, Naples, and England, where she worked in the court of King Charles. She became great friends with Galileo, and was the first woman artist in history to run her own large studio, complete with an army of assistants. Gentileschi's story is often framed by her rape, but the crux of her life wasn't what she endured, but what she created.

Dorothy Pitman Hughes & Gloria Steinem

Writers and activists, b.1938 and b.1934

Gloria Steinem and Dorothy Pitman Hughes, 1971.

> *'Feminism has never been about getting a job for one woman. It's about making life more fair for women everywhere'*
>
> Gloria Steinem

In a church basement in New York in March 1969, Gloria Steinem felt a click, an awakening. The event had been organised by the radical feminist group Redstockings, prompted by a New York legislative hearing on abortion law reform the month before, at which fourteen of the fifteen medical and psychiatric experts called to testify were men. The fifteenth was a nun. This gathering was different. Twelve speakers, all women, described their personal experiences of abortion before an audience of 300 men and women. This was four years before the landmark ruling in the case of Roe vs Wade, which struck down many of the legal barriers to abortion in the US.

Steinem experienced a 'great blinding lightbulb' as the women testified, recognition that she was not alone. She had had an abortion in London, aged 22, in the late 1950s, on her way to a fellowship in India. Her 2015 book *My Life on the Road* is dedicated to the doctor who performed it, who told her she must make two promises: never to tell anyone his name; and to do what she wanted with her life.

She was honouring this last promise in the late 1960s as a writer, living in Manhattan, with a regular New York magazine column called City Politic. The column she wrote following the abortion speak out, 'After Black Power, Women's Liberation', didn't reveal her feminist awakening, which her biographer Carolyn Heilbrun has described as 'the single most significant moment in Steinem's life'. Instead, it used the more objective tone expected of a serious writer at the time to describe the essential ferment of the women's liberation movement: the black-veiled brides who released mice into the Bridal Fair at Madison Square Garden, protesting the domesticity being marketed to women; the demonstration against Wall Street organised by WITCH – The Women's International Terrorist Conspiracy from Hell – which led to a spooky five point fall in the markets; and the students who had set up a Liberation School, offering a course on women as an oppressed class.

Over the next few years, Steinem would become perhaps the most famous feminist in the US. Unlike many of the feminists who made their names in the 1960s and 1970s – Betty Friedan, Kate Millett, Shulamith Firestone, Robin Morgan and Susan Brownmiller among them – this wasn't due to the publication of a landmark book, but resulted from a relentless speaking tour. 'To list the colleges and universities at which Steinem and her partners spoke would take many pages,' writes Heilbrun, 'perhaps more than to list those at which they did not speak.'

Steinem was first approached by a lecture bureau, asking her to speak about feminism, after her women's liberation column. She was intrigued, but terrified at the thought of public speaking. A solution was suggested by Dorothy Pitman (later Pitman Hughes), who Steinem met while interviewing her for City Politic in June 1969. Pitman Hughes ran a pioneering childcare centre in New York, committed to multiracial and non-sexist childrearing, and during the interview the two women had joined forces in an argument against a young Italian man who worked there, who said he wouldn't allow his girlfriend to have a job after marriage. The pair made the case for women's equality, and convinced him.

Pitman Hughes suggested they go on the road together, which quelled Steinem's fears. 'Right away,' Steinem writes in *My Life on the Road*, 'we discovered that a white woman and a black woman speaking together attracted far more diverse audiences than either one of us would have done on our own . . . Together and separately, we as speakers disproved another description used to disqualify feminists: that we were all 'whitemiddleclass,' a phrase used by the media then (and academics who believe those media clippings now) as if it were a single adjective to describe the women's movement. In fact, the first-ever nationwide poll of women's opinions on issues of gender equality showed that African-American women were twice as likely as white women to support them.'

Pitman Hughes had grown up in Lumpkin, Georgia, where her family worked at the local paper mill; one night, when she was a child, the Ku Klux Klan beat up her father, before leaving him on the front porch. 'I made the decision early on to change what I could,' Pitman Hughes has said, and she committed herself to addressing racism, classism and sexism, helping to organise buses for the March on Washington in 1963 (where Martin Luther King Jr gave his 'I Have a Dream' speech), getting to know Malcolm X, starting day care centres when she realised women were having to leave their children at home while they worked, and setting up a shelter for battered women. She has also spoken out strongly against gentrification.

In 1971, a portrait of Pitman Hughes and Steinem featured in *Esquire* magazine, their pose – both raising their right fist – modelled on the black power salute given by US athletes Tommie Smith and John Carlos at the 1968 Olympics. That same year, the pair were part of a group who met to discuss starting a new feminist magazine. The result was *Ms. Magazine*, which became a sensation, its first 300,000 copies selling out across the country in eight days. A special episode of *The David Frost Show* was made when it launched; it ended with Pitman Hughes and other women performing a song they had written especially.

After having a baby, Pitman Hughes decided to stop touring, and Steinem was joined at speaking events by the feminist lawyer Florynce Kennedy or editor and activist Margaret Sloan, both African-American women. 'As I talked to Gloria,' Pitman Hughes told Heilbrun, 'I started to see comradeship between my blackness and my femaleness, an expansion.' It was a friendship that led millions of women to experience for themselves the awakening that had changed Steinem's life.

Dorothea Lange

Documentary photographer, 1895–1965

Dorothea Lange in California, February 1936.

> *'The camera is a powerful instrument for saying to the world: this is the way it is. Look at it. Look at it'*

A woman in a migrant camp in California in 1936 holds a baby in her lap, two children flanking her, their faces turned away from the camera to rest on their mother's shoulders, as she leans forward, brow furrowed, face weather beaten and washed with anxiety. Her hand hovers at her chin.

Migrant Mother became the most influential of all the photographs taken as part of a US government project to document rural poverty during the Great Depression. Dorothea Lange was a staff photographer for the project, in her early forties, on her way home one day from a stint on the road when she saw a hand drawn sign for a pea-pickers' camp. An internal argument began, she told *Popular Photography* magazine in 1960. Surely she didn't need to stop? She was anxious for home, and the rain was beating heavily, but twenty miles down the road, 'following instinct, not reason,' she turned back.

The pea crops had frozen and around 3,000 people were starving and stranded. Lange approached 'the hungry and desperate mother, as if drawn by a magnet . . . She told me her age, that she was 32. She said that they had been living on frozen vegetables from the surrounding fields, and birds that the children killed. She had just sold the tyres from her car to buy food.'

Published in newspapers around the country, capturing the essence of the age, the photo became arguably the most famous in US history. More information gradually emerged about its subject. Her name was Florence Owens Thompson, and while the image had been understood to represent white rural poverty, she was actually Native American. Her family disputed elements of Lange's account – they had not sold their tyres – but came to appreciate the picture. When Thompson was ill and needed financial assistance towards the end of her life, an appeal mentioning the image led to a wave of donations.

Lange was born in Hoboken, New Jersey, and after her father left the family, she, her younger brother Martin and her mother went to live with her maternal grandmother. As a child, she contracted polio, and began walking with a limp. Lange's biographer, Linda Gordon, has said that when the photographer was teaching in the 1950s she would ask students to take a picture of 'what their lives were really about'. They challenged her to complete the assignment too, and she took her only ever self-portrait. It shows her stricken foot, twisted in the light.

In her early twenties, she left the East Coast with a friend, determined to travel the world. As described in the documentary *Grab a Hunk of Lightning*, they made it to San Francisco, where their money was stolen; Lange began working at a department store photography counter to get by. She had decided as a child to become a photographer, and had studied the works of Alfred Stieglitz and apprenticed for Arnold Genthe. Now she persuaded a backer to help her set up her own portrait studio.

Here she photographed San Francisco's wealthier citizens, and in the evenings it became a meeting place for the city's artists. She fell in love with painter, Maynard Dixon, 20 years her senior, and they married in 1920 and had two sons. Dixon was often away and Lange struggled to keep the family afloat.

By 1933, as the Great Depression deepened, Lange could see people queuing for food from her studio window. 'I set myself a big problem,' she said, years later. 'I would go down there, I would photograph, I would come back, develop, print, mount, and put the images on the wall, all in 24 hours, just to see if I could grab a hunk of lightning.' That first day she photographed a man in the breadline at a soup kitchen. He is leaning on a fence, facing the camera, holding an empty tin cup. *White Angel Breadline* encapsulated the era's poverty (when it was auctioned for $822,400 in 2005, it ironically became the most expensive twentieth-century photograph ever sold to that date).

In 1934, Lange photographed a longshoreman's strike on the San Francisco waterfront. Her work was seen by Paul Taylor, an economics professor at Berkeley, who had been documenting labourers contending with impossible conditions, and the pair began working together.

Lange's marriage to Dixon had long since broken down, and she and Taylor fell in love, and were married in December 1935; their drive to document the Great Depression was not easy for their children, who were sent out to board with foster families. What the pair found on the road was astonishing to Lange. They were among the first to notice the huge migration from the Dust Bowl, the parts of the country subject to dust storms, which had destroyed homes and livelihoods. In the 1930s she took images of sharecroppers and plantation owners, documenting the legacy of slavery.

Lange tended to shoot upwards, partly due to her short stature, making people's faces look monumental and imbuing them with dignity. Her images were a world away from most of those taken of the poor beforeor since.

In 1941, the Japanese attacked the US naval base at Pearl Harbour, and Franklin D. Roosevelt's government responded by ordering thousands of people of Japanese ancestry, two-thirds of them US citizens, from their homes in America, putting them in internment camps. Lange was commissioned to document this, to show the government wasn't torturing or persecuting the internees. What she saw horrified her, and when the US military eventually saw her photographs, they were impounded. It wasn't until 2006 that they were released as a book.

In her final years, Lange suffered greatly with illness, but still travelled the world, continuing her work with Taylor. She died of esophageal cancer while preparing a retrospective for the Museum of Modern Art in New York – the first woman photographer to be granted one.

Ada Lovelace

Computer scientist, 1815–1852

Portrait of Ada King, Countess of Lovelace, by
Margaret Sarah Carpenter, oil on canvas, 1835.

*'That brain of mine is
something more than
merely mortal; as time
will show'*

In 1842, Ada, Countess of Lovelace, embarked on a translation project. Her great friend Charles Babbage, a mathematician and inventor 24 years her senior, had been working for the best part of a decade on his idea for a calculating machine called the Analytical Engine – a leap forward from his earlier invention, the Difference Engine (neither machine had been built). In an attempt to publicise the idea, hopeful his machine might one day whirr to glorious life, he had travelled to Turin, where an engineer called Luigi Federico Menabrea heard him speak, and published a paper about the device in a Swiss journal. Lovelace decided to translate this for publication in Britain, and having done so, she informed Babbage. As he wrote in his autobiography, two decades later, he was surprised. 'I asked why she had not herself written an original paper on a subject with which she was so intimately acquainted?'

It was so unusual for women to publish scientific papers in this era that even the visionary Lovelace hadn't considered it, but she responded with characteristic energy to Babbage's suggestion that she annotate Menabrea's essay. Her response was eventually more than double the length of the essay itself, and in her Notes A to G she achieved extraordinary feats.

In Note A, she compared the Difference Engine and the Analytical Engine. The first was strictly a calculating machine, while the second had the potential, she saw, to be a general-purpose machine – Lovelace was conceptualising the modern computer for the first time, a century before the computer age began in earnest. Her understanding of the machine's capabilities went beyond anything Babbage had yet considered. 'It might act upon other things besides numbers,' she wrote, suggesting, for example, 'the engine might compose elaborate and scientific pieces of music of any degree of complexity'.

She also provided the first insight into how a computer might work: Note G features an algorithm, the first computer program ever published. And her breakthroughs continued in her thoughts on what we now know as artificial intelligence. Lovelace considered whether what would come to be called a computer might ever think for itself. She concluded it would not. 'The Analytical Engine has no pretensions whatever to "originate" anything,' she wrote. 'It can do whatever we know how to order it to perform. It can follow analysis; but it has no power of anticipating any analytical relations or truths.'

Lovelace was the child of the poet Lord Byron and his educated, wealthy wife Annabella Milbanke. Their marriage began in January 1815, Ada was born in December that year, and five weeks later Annabella left her husband. He had been described by his former lover Lady Caroline Lamb as 'mad, bad, and dangerous to know', and rumours of an incestuous relationship with his half-sister Augusta persisted after his marriage.

Ada never saw her father again. She was educated well from a young age – her mother's focus was on making her completely rational, to exorcise her father's poetic demons. In a letter to Byron, not long before his death in Greece in 1824, Annabella wrote that their daughter was 'not devoid of imagination, but is chiefly exercised in connection with her mechanical ingenuity – the manufacture of ships, boats, etc'.

This love of mechanics developed into a focus on flying when Lovelace was twelve, as described in James Essinger's book *A Female Genius*. In a letter to her mother in April 1828, she wrote about her plan to make a pair of wings for herself, proportionally the same size as a bird's. Five days later, she had decided instead to create a form in the shape of a horse, with a steam engine inside and an immense pair of wings – passengers could sit on its back. A few days later, she observed she had had great pleasure 'in looking at the wing of a dead crow and I still think that I shall manage to fly and I have thought of three different ways of flying that all strike me as likely'.

In 1829, Lovelace suffered temporary paralysis as a result of the measles, and was largely bed bound until 1832, but her education continued, and the next year came two auspicious events in quick succession. The first was her debut at court. The second was meeting Charles Babbage.

Their friendship involved deep discussion of Babbage's inventions and continued after her marriage to William King in 1835, and the birth of her three children. Lovelace's dedication to the subject is clear in a sixteen-page letter she wrote to Babbage after the completion of her Notes on Menabrea's essay. 'I give to *you* the *first* choice and offer of my services and my intellect,' she wrote. 'Do not lightly reject them'. She essentially offered to manage Babbage's affairs, to act as the promoter of his work on the Analytical Engine and attempt to take it beyond the realms of the conceptual. Babbage turned her down.

At 36, Lovelace died of uterine cancer. Her abilities as a scientist and mathematician have been questioned – there is a palpable sense, in some of the queries, that a woman couldn't possibly be capable of conceiving the modern computer and being at the forefront of technological history. As a result of the scepticism, Lovelace has become a guiding figure for some modern women scientists, whose capabilities are still too often questioned or denied. Walter Isaacson is clear about her contribution in his book *The Innovators*, in which he profiles the people who created the digital revolution, starting with a chapter on Lovelace. 'Ada's contribution was both profound and inspirational,' he writes. 'More than Babbage or any other person of her era, she was able to glimpse a future in which machines would become partners of the human imagination'.

Maya Angelou

Writer and teacher, 1928–2014

Maya Angelou on the beach in Pacific Palisades, California, 1988.

> **'Courage is the most important of all the virtues because without courage, you can't practice any other virtue consistently'**

For five years as a child, Maya Angelou stopped speaking. Aged eight, she was raped by her mother's boyfriend and brought to testify against him in court. The defence lawyer asked if the accused had touched her on any occasion before the rape, and afraid of having kept a previous incident secret (the rapist had said he would kill her big brother Bailey if she told anyone), she said no. The lie lumped in her throat, she wrote later, making it hard to breathe. The defendant was sentenced to a year and a day, but his lawyer secured his release that afternoon, and soon afterwards his body was found. He had apparently been kicked to death. Angelou felt her lie – which had actually cast the rapist in a slightly better light than he deserved – was to blame. 'The only thing I could do was to stop talking to people other than Bailey,' she wrote in her memoir *I Know Why the Caged Bird Sings*. 'If I talked to anyone else that person might die too.'

Angelou was eventually coaxed out of her mutism by a family friend, who encouraged her affinity with literature. She spent the rest of her life paying testament to the truth.

I Know Why the Caged Bird Sings was published when Angelou was in her early forties, the first of seven memoirs (she once joked that she wanted to be 'America's black female Proust'). The volumes describe her years as a high-achieving school pupil, a teenage mother, San Francisco's first black streetcar conductor, a sex worker and madam, part of a dance team with renowned choreographer Alvin Ailey, and a cast member for the opera *Porgy and Bess*. She was a calypso singer, a civil rights activist, and lived in Cairo, then Ghana, working as a journalist. 'Life loves the liver of it,' Angelou often said, and she honoured that outlook in full.

On her birthday in 1968, her friend Martin Luther King Jr was killed, plunging Angelou into a deep depression. She had gone to live in New York, determined to write, and at a dinner party with James Baldwin, she and the other guests told stories of their early years. An editor called Robert Loomis heard about her recollections, and suggested she become a memoirist. Angelou told him she wanted to be a playwright and poet, but he devised a strategy to convince her. 'You may be right not to attempt autobiography,' he said, 'because it is nearly impossible to write autobiography as literature. Almost impossible.' 'I'll start tomorrow,' said Angelou.

She would go to a hotel room to write, asking for the pictures to be removed from the walls, carrying yellow, lined legal notepads, a bottle of sherry, a Bible, thesaurus and deck of cards, in case she was minded to play solitaire. The books she wrote were loved, and influential. Earlier black women writers were 'frozen into self-consciousness by the need to defend black women and men against the vicious and prevailing stereotypes,' writes academic Mary Helen Washington, but Angelou wrote openly about her experiences of a deeply divided America.

I Know Why the Caged Bird Sings describes her early years with Bailey, her grandmother and Uncle Willie in the small Arkansas town of Stamps, where 'the segregation was so complete that most Black children didn't really, absolutely know what whites looked like. Other than that they were different, to be dreaded'. This was a world in which Angelou watched a group of white women attempt and fail to humiliate her proud, constant grandmother; and in which the threat of the Ku Klux Klan was such that, on one occasion at the family store, they had to clear a space in the onion and potato bins to hide Uncle Willie, who was physically disabled.

Her memoirs became part of the feminist canon. Angelou was asked in 1973 by interviewer Bill Moyers whether she considered the feminist movement 'a white woman's fantasy', and she replied that it was a necessity, before describing how race affected the experience of womanhood. 'A white man can run his society . . .' she said. 'The white American man makes the white American woman maybe not superfluous but just a little kind of decoration. Not really important to the turning around of the wheels. Well, the black American woman has never been able to feel that way. No black American man at any time in our history in the United States has been able to feel that he didn't need that black woman right against him, shoulder to shoulder . . . There is a kind of strength that is almost frightening in black women.'

Angelou was dizzyingly productive. In 1968, she wrote, produced and narrated a documentary series on the history of the blues. In 1971, she published her first poetry collection, *Just Give Me a Cool Drink of Water 'fore I Diiie*. It was nominated for a Pulitzer. In 1972, with the film *Georgia, Georgia*, she became the first black woman ever to have a screenplay produced, and wrote the soundtrack too. In 1973, she was nominated for a Tony award, for her Broadway appearance in *Look Away* (it closed after one night, so she clearly made that performance count). And in 1977, she played Kunta Kinte's grandmother in TV miniseries *Roots*. She was nominated for an Emmy.

She became a professor at Wake Forest University in North Carolina in 1981, and within three months had a revelation: 'I realised I was not a writer who teaches, but a teacher who writes.'

Angelou became America's teacher. At Bill Clinton's inauguration in 1993, she read her poem 'On the Pulse of Morning', with its lines: 'History, despite its wrenching pain, cannot be unlived, but if faced with courage, need not be lived again'. Angelou knew this was true of her own life, and hoped it could be true of a culture and a country too.

Björk

Musician, b.1965

Björk in London, 1993.

'If it's not dangerous,
it's not worth doing'

On an October day in 1993, Björk stood on the back of a flatbed truck, in a shimmering dress, being driven through New York. Her song 'Big Time Sensuality' was playing through loudspeakers, and people were dancing in the streets, while Björk danced too, laughing and skipping, singing the lyrics: 'I can sense it / Something important is about to happen / It's coming up / It takes courage, to enjoy it / The hardcore and the gentle / Big time sensuality'. Her voice moved from guttural growls to soprano swoops, and the camera moved in close as her face broke into an ecstatic grin.

The song featured on the album *Debut*, released in 1993, when Björk was in her late twenties. She'd started attending music school, aged five, in her home country, Iceland; her first album was released when she was eleven. Decade after decade Björk has remained consistently creative and innovative. As a child, she created beats from a recording of her grandfather's snores, and used a popcorn machine as a drum accompaniment; as an adult she has produced music that weaves pop, punk, classical, jazz, hip hop and choral music. Her 2001 tour for the album *Vespertine* included a 54-piece orchestra, the electronic duo Matmos, a harpist and a choir from Greenland. Her 2004 album *Medúlla* was almost entirely a cappella; she told the writer Alex Ross that her aim was to explore 'every noise that a throat makes'. For the 2011 album *Biophilia*, which was conceived around the interaction of nature and technology, new musical instruments were made.

Björk has acted too, appearing in Lars von Trier's 2000 film *Dancer in the Dark*, for which she won Best Actress at the Cannes Film Festival, and throughout her career she has created brilliant imagery, exploding the expected depiction of women in pop. In her first video as a solo artist, 'Human Behaviour' (1993), directed by Michel Gondry, she was adrift in a fairytale woodland, along with a bear, a hunter and a hedgehog. Spike Jonze's video for her reworking of the Betty Hutton song 'It's Oh So Quiet' (1995) was a play on Hollywood musicals, a world in which ordinary people break into song and dance in formation. For 'All is Full of Love' (1999), directed by Chris Cunningham, she became a matching pair of robots, techno-Björks embracing each other as machines whirred around them. And for 'Who Is It' (2004), she wore a dress, designed by Alexander McQueen, shaped like a bell, covered in thousands of smaller bells, the embodiment of sound.

Björk's artistic guts and stamina are rooted in Iceland, where she was born to a mother who was a feminist activist, and a father who became the leader of the country's union of electricians. Her parents split up when she was small, and her mother's second husband was a rock musician; they lived communally with other families when Björk was growing up. 'I was never the cheerleader at school,' she once said. 'I was always the kid at the back of the class with the spiders in her pockets.'

She threw this unusual energy into music. There was the pop album at eleven, a flute composition called 'Glora' at fifteen, and a series of bands, including an all-girl punk group called Spit and Snot, while still in her teens. The best known of her punk bands was Kukl; she told writer Paul Lester that it was with them she 'took the biggest musical bungee jumps'. The band's front man was Einar Orn – during shows he would pull a cord around his neck until he fainted – and he was also involved in the band which gave Björk her first taste of international stardom, The Sugarcubes. She and her friends formed a record label and collective called Bad Taste in 1986, with the manifesto: 'Bad Taste will use every imaginable and unimaginable method, e.g. inoculation, extermination, tasteless advertisements and announcements, distribution and sale of common junk and excrement.' The Sugarcubes were set up to mock a particular kind of Icelandic pop breeziness, but with their songs 'Birthday' and 'Hit', they began appearing in the charts internationally.

In 1990, Björk made an album of jazz standards, *Gling-Gló*, and a few years later came her breakthrough with *Debut*. It's tempting to try to place her in musical history, to trace her relationship to Joni Mitchell, for instance, whose albums *Hejira*, and *Don Juan's Reckless Daughter* influenced her in her teens; or to Kate Bush, whose *The Dreaming* appears in her eclectic list of favourite records.

Björk has said of Mitchell that she loved her because, 'She was creating her own universe; she wasn't a guest in a man's world'. The same goes for her. But that hasn't stopped people misattributing her work. She spoke about this in an interview with Jessica Hopper in 2015, remarking on how often her work on the production of her albums was credited to male producers who had come in for a few weeks at the end of the process. When the producers tried to clear this up with journalists or on social media, they went unheard; the misattribution was repeated. 'I want to support young girls who are in their twenties now,' Björk said, 'and tell them: "You're not just imagining things." It's tough. Everything that a guy says once, you have to say five times . . . After being the only girl in bands for ten years, I learned – the hard way – that if I was going to get my ideas through, I was going to have to pretend that they – men – had the ideas. I became really good at this and I don't even notice it myself. I don't really have an ego. I'm not that bothered. I just want the whole thing to be good.'

Katharine Hepburn

Film star, 1907–2003

Katharine Hepburn in the film *Keeper of the Flame*,
Hollywood, California, 1942.

> *'I have no fear of death. Must be wonderful, like a long sleep. But let's face it: it's how you live that really counts.'*

Katharine Hepburn represented a new kind of woman on screen, 'more modern than tomorrow!' whooped the film magazines. She was strong, courageous and athletic, and known too for her screwball humour and extraordinary voice. Many stars of the early talking pictures adopted a mid-Atlantic accent, blending British and American vowels, but no one had a voice as distinctive as Hepburn's, so airily elevated and appealing.

Her voice drew on her Connecticut childhood, born into a privileged and progressive family. Thomas Norval Hepburn, her father, was a doctor who specialised in the treatment of venereal disease, while her mother, Katharine Houghton Hepburn, became a women's rights activist within months of her daughter's birth. In her 1991 memoir, *Me*, Hepburn recalls blowing up 'VOTES FOR WOMEN' balloons in purple, white and green – the suffragette colours – when she was eight, and visitors to the family home included British suffragette leader Emmeline Pankhurst and Margaret Sanger, who opened the first birth control clinic in the US.

As a child, Hepburn fervently wanted to be a boy. 'With one brother Tom older and my two younger, Dick and Bob, being a girl was a torment,' she wrote. 'I'd always wanted to be a boy. Jimmy was my name, if you want to know.' She developed a love of sports, and writes that she was, 'skinny and very strong and utterly fearless'. She and her siblings (there were two sisters too) were well aware of their good fortune; the word 'lucky' punctuates her autobiography.

The idyll was broken by Tom's death when she was fourteen. The siblings were staying with a family friend in New York, when Tom hanged himself; Hepburn found the body. Her father described this as 'a deplorable accident' and in William J. Mann's biography of Hepburn, he writes that she, 'clung quite stubbornly to the belief that it was accidental'. Sadly, a death wish seemed to run through the male line of the family on both sides, with Hepburn's maternal grandfather and great uncle having killed themselves, as did her father's oldest brother. Within days of Tom's death, another of her father's brothers also died by his own hand.

Hepburn withdrew, but went on to study at the women's college, Bryn Mawr, and decided she would act. Her first stage experiences would have deterred a weaker temperament. She was fired from her first play, *The Big Pond*, after one performance. Her appearance in *Death Takes a Holiday* ended when she was told she was being given 'the privilege of resigning from the cast'. If they wanted to fire her, they should, she said. They did. In *The Animal Kingdom*, opposite Leslie Howard, she tried to 'tame down my too vivid personality', as she became aware of Howard's distaste for her. She was fired again.

Then came *The Warrior's Husband*, in which she arrived onstage in a metal link tunic, shin guards, helmet and cape, carrying a shield, a stag draped over one shoulder. The audience applauded her entrance and, she wrote later, 'I was just full of the joy of life and opportunity and a wild desire to be absolutely fascinating'.

Soon she was starring in her first film, *A Bill of Divorcement* (1932). The firings stopped. She won her first best actress Oscar in 1934, for *Morning Glory*, and was a huge success as Jo in *Little Women* (1933). Hepburn became known for her style, and specifically for wearing trousers when this was genuinely subversive. Speaking to the magazine *Ladies' Home Journal* in 1975, she remarked, 'I've dressed this way for 40 years, just because I had brains enough to know that certain kinds of shoes were comfortable and keeping up stockings is uncomfortable.'

The look was influential. But it was also probably one of the factors that led to her topping the 'box office poison' list of actors in 1938. She had suffered a few flops, including a stint on Broadway in *The Lake*, which led Dorothy Parker to quip that she 'ran the gamut of emotions from A to B'. Another play, *The Philadelphia Story*, saved her career. Her partner at the time, entrepreneur Howard Hughes, bought the screen rights, and soon she was starring in the film alongside Cary Grant and James Stewart.

Hepburn plays Tracy Lord in *The Philadelphia Story*, an heiress variously described as a statue, a prig, a marvellous distant queen, a perennial spinster and a virgin goddess. The story concerns the melting of her icy carapace, and as Hepburn's friend, writer Garson Kanin, once remarked, this became the formula for her most successful films: a stuck-up woman 'is brought down to earth by an earthy type, or a lowbrow . . . or a cataclysmic situation'. The first film in which she co-starred with Spencer Tracy, *Woman of the Year* (1942), involved the pair sparring, as a result of her character's commitment to her work as a political columnist, before a famous scene where she gives in and makes him a botched breakfast. But it is always Hepburn's vigour and wilfulness that persists in the memory. As film critic Molly Haskell once said, in assessing her standing as a feminist icon, 'to give the last word to her compromises, on screen and off, seems perverse'.

Tracy had been sceptical about starring alongside her, reportedly asking: 'How can I do a picture with a woman who has dirt under her fingernails and who is of ambiguous sexuality and always wears pants?' Then he saw *The Philadelphia Story*. The pair appeared in nine films together, and had a romance lasting 26 years. There were twelve Oscar nominations for Hepburn, including four wins, and she sailed on, an icon of women's independence. In her autobiography she writes, 'what a tremendous opportunity it is just to be alive. The potential', and in 1952, critic Kenneth Tynan echoed this, writing that, 'Her very nerve ends tingle with glee: she is an affirmation of life . . . Hepburn is a gay byproduct of female emancipation, wearing the pants and using the vote, and her aggressiveness is that of the sun at high noon'. She embodied, beautifully, a life wish.

Diana Nyad

Swimmer, b.1949

Diana Nyad, 1974.

> **'I learned at a tender age
> that life is too short to fill
> with unobsessed time'**

In August 2009, the month of her 60th birthday, Diana Nyad decided to pursue a dream she had abandoned three decades earlier, an adventure no one had ever completed: to swim from Cuba to Florida without a shark cage. She had tried the swim herself, aged 28, when she was among the best long distance swimmers in the world. In 1978, her attempt was made in a shark cage, and on the way she faced eight foot waves, severe seasickness, minor jellyfish stings all over her body, and a serious sting from a Portuguese man o' war. Then there was the chafing (ocean swimmers can 'chafe to a severity of third-degree burns' she writes in her 2015 memoir *Find a Way*). She braved the physical and mental exhaustion, the psychological extremity of being awake for the days it would take to swim 103 miles, only to be told, almost 42 hours in, that they had been blown so far off course they were heading for Texas, 800 miles away. She had lost 29 pounds already.

Nyad was keen to try again in 1979, but was denied entry to Cuba. Instead, she decided to end her swimming career with a Bahamas to Florida crossing, and the day before her 30th birthday completed the 102.5 mile swim, establishing a world distance record. Her Cuba to Florida dream had become, as she writes, just 'a whisper of unfinished business'.

Nyad was five when she first considered becoming a swimmer. Aris, the man she has always considered her father (at college, she learned he was her stepfather) told her Nyad meant a girl or woman champion swimmer, and 'what I heard was the word 'champion'' she writes. Aris was charismatic, a storyteller, and con man, who was also violent; on one occasion he hit her mother so hard that Nyad and her siblings thought he had broken her cheekbone.

Five years later, Nyad's geography teacher, a former Olympic swimmer himself, announced that any child who tried out for the swimming team would get an A in geography. As she swam laps the next day, he told her she was going to be the best swimmer in the world. It was the start of her athletic career. 'Even as a ten-year-old,' she writes, 'I was getting up at four-thirty every morning, 365 days a year, no alarm clock needed. A thousand sit-ups and fifty chin-ups every day. Never 999, never 49.'

Aris and her swimming coach both sexually assaulted her, separately, on a number of occasions, and when she became a marathon swimmer in her mid-twenties, she often swam 'in utter rage', she writes. Long distance swimming is masochistic, fraught with potential hypothermia, hallucinations, vomiting, excruciating boredom and dehydration. She started swimming marathons against male and female competitors, before taking on epic solo swims, making her name with her journey around Manhattan Island. In July 1927, Californian swimmer Byron Summers took eight hours 56 minutes to swim around the island. On 6 October 1977, well-wishers crowding the streets above her, Nyad broke his record, with a time of seven hours 57 minutes.

After giving up swimming, Nyad became a sportscaster and journalist, travelling the world, telling other people's stories. But at 60, her own story became wildly compelling again. The Australian swimmer Susie Maroney had made the Cuba to Florida crossing in 1997 – but with the aid of a shark cage. Nyad was determined to swim in open water.

She began training, and building a team including medics, navigators and managers, as well as experts on the weather, and shark and jellyfish behaviour. Her second attempt, on 7 August 2011, ended with an asthma attack after 29 hours.

Almost seven weeks later, 23 September 2011, she tried again. Two hours in, she was attacked by box jellyfish. The pain is 'otherworldly,' she writes. 'My entire body as if dipped in hot burning oil.' Her breathing became constricted, and she had the sensation of spinal paralysis. She kept swimming, but was stung again later. Nyad left the water for a few hours for treatment, before returning to the precise spot where she'd emerged, hoping to complete this as a 'staged' swim. She remained in the water for 44 hours and thirty minutes, before finishing the attempt; the log of medication administered to her over those two days ran to four single-spaced pages.

Her fourth attempt, in August 2012, was also marred by jellyfish stings, and a severe tropical storm. After 51 hours, lightning strikes made it too dangerous for the shark diving team to continue.

Many of Nyad's team believed she should give up. There had been four attempts, all wholehearted, all unsuccessful. Steven Munatones, director of the World Open

Water Swimming Association, put the chance of anyone completing the crossing at 2 per cent.

But on 31 August 2013, she made the leap into the waters off Havana. She now had a suit and mask to protect her from jellyfish stings, an outfit which Munatones described as like 'wearing lead shoes to walk up Mount Everest'. During the first night she vomited into the mask, and the retainer she was wearing over her teeth led to lacerations and swelling in her mouth, making it difficult to eat and drink. She became delirious, hallucinating the Taj Mahal, and then, in the ocean below her, the Yellow Brick Road, with the Seven Dwarfs walking along it.

But for all the journey's impossibilities, everything – currents, weather conditions – was on her side. Nyad completed the swim on 2 September 2013, 110.86 miles in almost 53 hours, 35 years after her first attempt. She was 64. On taking up long distance swimming, she writes, she was 'looking to be a person who never, ever gives up'. Few have honoured their promise so powerfully.

Françoise Barré-Sinoussi

Virologist, b.1947

Françoise Barré-Sinoussi in her laboratory at the
Pasteur Institute in Paris, October 2008.

'My colleagues sometimes say I am an activist, and that is the best compliment'

Not long before she finished her PhD, in the mid-1970s, Françoise Barré-Sinoussi met with a senior staff member at the Pasteur Institute in Paris to discuss continuing her work there. He was not encouraging. She had been interning at the Institute since the late 1960s, dedicating many hours to the lab, but years later she recalled him telling her: 'A woman in science, they never do anything. They are only good at caring for the home and babies. Forget this dream.'

She ignored the advice and decided to show him what a woman in science could do. Born into a French family of modest means, Barré-Sinoussi had chosen a natural sciences degree over medicine, partly because the course would be shorter and less expensive, and she was now determined to pursue her ambitions in the male-dominated world of medical research. She considered herself part of the generation that protested across France in 1968, rallying against establishment values. 'It was a period of activism and women were demanding their rights,' she once said. 'I was not out demonstrating on the streets, but I shared a lot of those ideas.' She would go on not just to work at the Pasteur Institute, but to make a historic breakthrough there, and set up her own laboratory.

At the start of her career, there were two offers of work – she could concentrate on how alcohol affected the liver, or focus on cancer. A young cousin of hers had died of leukaemia, so she opted for the latter. In a laboratory in the Paris suburbs, she began the work on retroviruses which would change the course of history.

By 1983 she was working on a team led by Luc Montagnier at the Pasteur Institute, when they were approached by the infectious disease specialist, Willy Rozenbaum. He asked them to look for a retrovirus in a disease called AIDS. At the time, around 50 people in France were known to be infected, and Rozenbaum gave the researchers a lymph node sample from one of these patients in January 1983. Just fifteen days later came the breakthrough. They had identified the HIV virus, a discovery that had immediate and brilliant implications. Within a few years a diagnostic test had been developed, and the laboratory had decoded the HIV genome. Their work enabled blood donations to be screened for the virus, which stopped people being infected through transfusions, and soon the first generation of antiretroviral drugs would be trialled too – treatments that eventually allowed people to live with HIV as a chronic condition, rather than a fatal one.

It's clear Barré-Sinoussi feels deeply for the HIV and AIDS patients she has met. A year after the discovery of the HIV virus, she travelled to the US to give a talk at the General Hospital in San Francisco, a trip she described three decades later in an extensive interview with journalist Patrick Strudwick. One of the doctors asked if she would meet a patient who was in the emergency room, and she agreed. The man was so ill that he struggled even to speak, but she could just make out his thanks, and when she asked him why he was thanking her, he said, 'Not for me, for the others'. A few hours later, he died. 'Since that day,' Barré-Sinoussi told Strudwick, 'I still have that image in my mind . . . He took my hand and I still feel his hand in my hand today.'

While the discovery of the virus was very exciting, Barré-Sinoussi has said, 'as a human being, it was really awful. At that time, AIDS was really a tragedy. People were dying. They were young, dying of this new disease, and knowing as a scientist that it would probably take time, too much time for many of them to benefit from any treatment that science could deliver was really very, very stressful'.

She believes scientists sometimes have to be activists, and has spoken out against repressive laws around the world – those which criminalise gay sex and intravenous drug use, for instance – for pushing these behaviours under-ground, and encouraging the spread of disease. In 2008, she and Montagnier won the Nobel Prize for their discovery of HIV, with the committee noting that 'never before has science and medicine been so quick to discover, identify the origin and provide treatment for a new disease entity'. A year after this worldwide recognition, Barré-Sinoussi took advantage of her high profile to write an open letter to Pope Benedict XVI, criticising his assertion that the distribution of condoms helped spread disease.

In 1988, Barré-Sinoussi opened her own lab at the Pasteur Institute; she retired in 2015. Towards the end of her career, asked for the advice she would give young scientists, she replied: 'the primary motivation must be the advancement of science for the benefit of human health. If they pursue a career just for themselves, when they get to the end of the road they might not feel like they have accomplished what they set out to do.' Useful advice for almost anybody.

Chimamanda Ngozi Adichie

Writer, b.1977

Chimamanda Ngozi Adichie at the 2012 Hay Festival,
Hay-on-Wye, Wales.

> *'Try and create the*
> *world you want*
> *to live in'*

When Chimamanda Ngozi Adichie published her first novel, *Purple Hibiscus*, in 2003, a journalist in Nigeria took her to one side. She should know, he warned, that people had been calling it a feminist book. One of its central characters, Eugene, is controlling and violent towards his family, including his 15-year-old daughter, the book's narrator, Kambili, and his story does not end positively. The journalist's 'advice to me – he was shaking his head sadly as he spoke – was that I should never call myself a feminist,' writes Adichie, 'since feminists are women who are unhappy because they cannot find husbands'.

This story is recounted in *We Should All Be Feminists*, a book based on a talk Adichie gave in 2012 which has arguably encouraged more people to consider feminism, and to consider calling themselves a feminist, than any other text in history. Its reach has been extraordinary. The original talk has been watched online by millions, and many more have heard Adichie speaking on Beyoncé's song 'Flawless', a sample which ends with this definition of the word feminist: 'a person who believes in the social, political, and economic equality of the sexes.' In 2015 it was announced that the essay would be distributed to every 16-year-old girl and boy in Sweden.

We Should All Be Feminists uses personal stories to elegantly delineate the ways in which gender constitutes a class system. Adichie writes about an incident at primary school, for instance, when her teacher told the students that whoever came first in a test would be made class monitor. She studied hard, aced the test, only to be told that the monitor had to be a boy; the second-placed student won the prize. Other slights arrived in adulthood, including the man who thanked her male companion for a cash tip Adichie had given – it was supposed that, as a woman, she couldn't possibly be of independent means. She writes about the assumption that a woman alone in a hotel must be a sex worker, and about the ways in which men are taught to be hard, leaving them 'with *very* fragile egos. The *harder* a man feels compelled to be, the weaker his ego is. And then we do a much greater disservice to girls, because we raise them to cater to the fragile egos of males'.

Adichie was born in Enugu, in south-eastern Nigeria, the fifth of six children – her father a professor of statistics at the University of Nigeria, her mother the university's first female registrar. As a stellar student, there was an expectation that she would pursue medicine, and she did so for a short while in Nigeria, before swapping to pharmacy, and then leaving for the US aged nineteen. In a commencement address to students at Wellesley College in 2015, she said she had decided that, since she was expected to pursue medicine, she would 'become a psychiatrist and that way I could use my patients' stories for my fiction. But after one year of medical school I fled. I realised I would be a very unhappy doctor and I really did not want to be responsible for the inadvertent death of my patients'. She won a scholarship to study in the US, and went on to complete a postgraduate degree in creative writing.

In 1997 she published a collection of poetry, *Decisions*, and the next year a play, *For Love of Biafra*. *Purple Hibiscus* was shortlisted for the Orange Prize for Fiction and her next novel *Half of a Yellow Sun* (2006), set in the late 1960s during the Biafran War in Nigeria, went on to win it in 2007. Both Adichie's mother and father had lost their own fathers during the war, and her father's family lost everything they owned. She has talked of the pressure she felt to ensure the novel captured the conflict correctly and Chinua Achebe said of the book: 'we do not usually associate wisdom with beginners, but here is a new writer endowed with the gift of ancient storytellers.'

Her acclaimed novel *Americanah* (2013) considers race in the US through the eyes of a character, Ifemelu, who, like Adichie herself, travelled from Nigeria to the US to study. Strong, complicated female characters are central to her work, and in that Wellesley speech, she urged the graduating class of women to consider carefully what they create. 'Write television shows in which female strength is not depicted as remarkable but merely normal . . .' she said. 'Campaign and agitate for paid paternity leave everywhere in America. Hire more women where there are few. But remember that a woman you hire doesn't have to be exceptionally good. Like a majority of the men who get hired, she just needs to be good enough.' When that last observation comes true, the world will shake on its axis. And it will do so partly because of women such as Adichie, who don't heed the warning against feminism – but instead explain, carefully and compellingly, why we should all be feminists.

Elizabeth Garrett Anderson

Doctor, 1836–1917

Elizabeth Garrett Anderson, c. 1889.

When Elizabeth Garrett Anderson told her parents she wanted to study medicine, her father Newson responded with disgust, while her mother Louisa said it was a disgrace, started crying, and shut herself in her bedroom. Family and friends expressed concern for Garrett Anderson's health. In the mid-1800s, it was thought the strain, for a woman, of entering such a profession meant a breakdown was assured, an early grave likely.

Garrett Anderson faced other difficulties. Women of her era weren't eligible to train at medical school, they were barred from most medical qualifications, and weren't allowed to join the British Medical Association. There were no qualified women doctors in Britain, and hadn't been for centuries.

But she was determined, and not just for her own sake. 'No one has time for everything,' she once said, 'the passion of my life is to help women'.

Garrett Anderson was born into a family of relatively modest means, her first home a pawnshop in Whitechapel, and when she was five the family moved to Aldeburgh, in Suffolk. Their fortunes changed with Newson's purchase of a barley and coal merchant's business, and when Garrett

Anderson was thirteen she attended boarding school for a few years. She had nine siblings, and for almost a decade after leaving school she lived at home, looking after the family estate, which now included an ice-house, piggeries, a Turkish bath and large garden. Domestic life frustrated her. As Jo Manton writes in her biography of Garrett Anderson, she once remarked that as a young woman, 'I was full of energy and vigour and of the discontent which goes with unemployed activities . . . Everything seemed wrong to me'.

Aged eighteen she met Emily Davies, who became a lifelong friend, and they had a conversation which has passed into legend. The pair were sitting by the fire in Garrett Anderson's family home, with one of her younger siblings, Millicent. 'Well Elizabeth, it is clear what has to be done,' said Davies. 'I must devote myself to securing higher education, while you open the medical profession for women. After these things are done we must see about getting the vote. You are younger than we are, Millie, so you must attend to that.' Davies co-founded Girton College, Cambridge, the first college in England to educate women, while Millicent led the non-militant wing of the campaign for women's suffrage.

The organised women's movement in Britain began in 1858, writes Manton, with publication of *The Englishwoman's Journal*, which focused on women's need for employment. The Society for Promoting the Employment of Women was set up in the journal's offices, and Garrett Anderson joined, attending an 1859 lecture by Dr Elizabeth Blackwell, the first woman to graduate from medical school in the US. Meeting Blackwell afterwards, she was surprised to be addressed as a future colleague. The seed of her career was planted.

Newson Garrett came around, accompanying her to Harley Street to meet some of the country's top doctors.

One asked why she couldn't be a nurse. 'Because I prefer to earn a thousand rather than twenty pounds a year,' she replied.

Garrett Anderson started her training with six months as a nurse at Middlesex Hospital, and afterwards it was agreed she could attend chemistry lectures and be allowed into the dissection room. She hoped to gain full admission to medical school. But in June 1861, as she and some male students were shown around the ward by a doctor, her progress faltered. They paused by a patient's bed, and the doctor asked a question. The male students were silent, and Garrett Anderson stepped in with the answer. Her male peers had been willing to accept or at least ignore her presence when they saw her as an oddity, but her growing ability and confidence was a threat to their pride.

The students wrote to the medical school authorities to explain why women should not be admitted to study alongside men. This was a dangerous innovation, they wrote; lecturers would surely self censor important medical information with a woman in the room. Presumably worried that they would lose their male students (and their fees), the authorities ruled that women would not be able to attend lectures.

The medical schools wouldn't teach her, and the examining bodies wouldn't examine her – Oxford, Cambridge, Edinburgh, Glasgow and the Royal College of Surgeons all refused Garrett Anderson's application. She finally had a positive response from the Society of Apothecaries, and with private tutoring and public lectures, obtained a licence to practice medicine (known as an LSA). She was the first woman in Britain to complete a recognised course of medical training and qualify as a doctor.

She set up her own practice, and a dispensary for the poor in Marylebone. The first patients were local women and children with varied ailments, but she began to see women from across London with gynaecological complaints, and decided to set up a new venture, staffed entirely by women. In February 1872, The New Hospital for Women opened.

Garrett Anderson was the first woman to be elected to the newly formed London School Board; the first female doctor of medicine in France (she gained her MD at the Sorbonne, completing her examinations in French); and the first woman mayor in England, elected in Aldeburgh in 1908.

She married James George Skelton Anderson in 1871 and the couple had three children. Throughout her life, she supported the constitutional movement for women's suffrage, but in 1908 she became involved with the militant movement, joining the Women's Social and Political Union, headed by Emmeline Pankhurst. She appeared at demonstrations, speaking about the importance of employment and political representation for women.

Garrett Anderson broke with the militants in 1912, believing their tactics were damaging their cause, and spent her last years in Aldeburgh. Her determination had opened a door. In 1876, eleven years after she qualified, an act was passed permitting women in Britain to enter the medical profession.

Gurinder Chadha

Film director, b.1960

Gurinder Chadha at the *Bend it Like Beckham* press conference,
Beverly Hills, California, 2003.

As a young woman, living for a year in India, Gurinder Chadha had a revelation. She was reading a feminist magazine, a discussion of media images, and realised she wanted to change how women like her were seen. 'My whole entry into the world of film and television and radio, was really me trying to make people like me visible,' she said in a radio interview, years later. 'Our stories weren't there. People who looked like me and thought like me weren't really visible on the screen in any shape or form, and so I tried to find a way to make that happen'.

Her debut film, *Bhaji on the Beach* (1993), was the first full-length feature film to be made by a British Asian woman, and Chadha has said that she and Meera Syal, who wrote the screenplay, imagined they'd never have the chance to make another one, so decided to explore every issue they felt was important. It's the story of an Asian women's group from Birmingham, on a day trip to the Blackpool seaside, and weaves the perspectives of women young and old, traditional and progressive, first and second generation immigrants, including experiences of racism, domestic violence, mixed race relationships, an unintended pregnancy, drunken kissing on Blackpool Pier and an unexpected encounter with a group of male strippers. It brought Chadha immediate recognition, and was nominated for Best British Film at the Baftas.

But there followed a fallow period of five years, at the end of which she decided to write the most commercial film she could, featuring an Indian girl at its heart. *Bend It Like Beckham* (2002), became the highest-grossing British-financed film in UK box-office history; it is also reportedly the first western film ever released in every country in the world, including North Korea. Its commercial success and reach reflect the universal essence of the story. A young woman wants to succeed as a footballer, a pursuit usually associated with men. One or both of her parents disapproves. She finds a way to succeed, and eventually her parents come around. This was the story of the central character, Jess, who is of Indian heritage, but also of her friend and fellow footballer, Jules. The story emphasised the similarities in people's experiences, beyond race and religion.

The warm, complicated relationship between Jess and her father was inspired by Chadha's relationship with her own father, who had died not long before filming began. The family came to Britain in 1962, when Chadha was a toddler; she was born in Kenya, where her father worked at Barclays Bank. When he enquired after similar employment at Barclays in Southall, west London, they took one look at the beard and turban traditional to all Sikh men, and threw him out. He went on to become a postman, but had to take off his turban to do so.

The far right racism of the National Front was on the rise in the UK when Chadha was growing up, and she became politicised in her teens, and frustrated by the low expectations of her at school. She went on to do a degree in development studies, before working as a BBC news reporter and documentary maker, then embarking on her film career.

Chadha's achievements are a reminder of how much one person can achieve in changing the media landscape, if they care strongly about representation. Film and TV has benefited from many women who have been committed to improving the representation of their own sex on screen, including, for instance, Shonda Rhimes, the writer and show runner who, with *Grey's Anatomy*, made a drama noted from the start for the diversity of its cast. With *Scandal*, in 2012, Rhimes created the first network drama with an African-American woman in the leading role since 1974, and this was soon followed, in 2014, by her show *How To Get Away With Murder* – its cast led by another African-American woman.

In her book *The Year of Yes* (2015), Rhimes emphasises what is at stake for those she has termed F.O.Ds – 'First. Only. Different'. As her shows became more popular, she writes, she was always aware, that 'this wasn't just my shot. It was *ours*. I had to do everything right. I had to keep it all afloat . . . If the first network drama with an African-American leading lady in 37 years didn't find an audience, who knows how long it would take for another to come along? Failure meant two generations of actresses might have to wait for another chance to be seen as more than a sidekick'.

If you change how women are portrayed on screen, you might just change the expectations women and girls have of their lives. Actor Geena Davis, star of feminist film classic *Thelma and Louise* (1991), decided to sponsor the largest ever research project on gender in children's entertainment after noticing how underrepresented women and girls were in the TV shows and films she was watching with her daughter. The findings were that for every female character in a family film, there are three male characters; the ratio of male-female characters has been the same since 1946; and crowd and group scenes in family films contain only 17 per cent female characters. In an essay for *The Hollywood Reporter*, Davis made two modest proposals for fixing this. One was that filmmakers could go through their projects and give some of the male characters women's names. The other was that, when describing a crowd in a script, screenwriters should simply specify: 'a crowd gathers, which is half female.'

The key to changing the representation of women on screen, according to Chadha, is to ignore the obstacles. 'If you were to sit back and go, you know what, this is against me, this is against me, this is against me, you wouldn't get anywhere.' Spoken like a true pioneer.

Ida B. Wells

Activist and journalist, 1862–1931

Ida B. Wells, 1920.

*'The way to right
wrongs is to turn
the light of truth
upon them'*

On her way home to Memphis in 1883, Ida B. Wells bought a first class rail ticket. She proceeded to the Ladies carriage, where only women and their male companions were allowed, and she could travel without the attentions of single men.

The conductor told her to move: he wouldn't allow a black woman to ride in first class. Wells refused to give up her seat, just as Rosa Parks would, 72 years later, in one of the defining protests of the civil rights movement.

The conductor left, then returned, repeating his instruction and moving Wells's bags to the smoking carriage. He grabbed her arm, trying to move her forcibly. Wells sank her teeth into his hand, and only when two more men joined him did they succeed in moving her.

She filed a lawsuit against the railroad for assault and discrimination, and won, awarded $500. But this led to a racist outcry, and her victory was overturned by the Tennessee State Supreme Court, with the rail company lawyer questioning Wells's right to call herself a lady. She ended up liable for court costs of $200.

Wells wrote about the case, and this marked the start of an extraordinary career as an activist and journalist that would make her, for a time, the most famous black woman in the US.

Born into slavery in 1862, Wells was three years old when the ratification of the Thirteenth Amendment formally abolished the slave trade. Her parents were skilled urban labourers and, as Mia Bay writes in her biography of Wells, *To Tell the Truth Freely*, they were 'intent on remaking themselves and their children as free people'. Wells grew up a passionate reader, and in the mid-1870s attended Rust College.

This period of study ended when yellow fever swept Wells's hometown of Holly Springs, killing her parents and baby brother Stanley. She was head of the family, aged sixteen, and was determined to keep her five younger siblings together, supporting them by teaching.

Aged nineteen, she moved to Memphis with her two youngest sisters and continued to teach; after the article about her protest she continued to write too. There were only 45 black female journalists in the US in the 1880s, writes Bay, and Wells became well known by her pen name: Iola, Princess of the Press. In 1889, while still a teacher, she bought a one-third interest in a newspaper called *The Memphis Free Speech and Headlight* and became editor – she was the first woman in US history to own and edit a black newspaper. She made it a commercial success, which proved fortunate when Wells lost her teaching job, after writing an article which criticised the conditions in Memphis's black schools.

The courage to write the truth, whatever the consequences, was essential to her next move: investigating lynching. Between 1882 and 1930 lynching was responsible for the deaths of more than 3,220 African-Americans, and as Bay writes, this white-on-black mob violence 'was so popular in the South that it was commemorated in postcards featuring the dead black bodies hanging from trees, bridges, and streetlights'. Until Wells took it on, it went almost unchallenged.

Her campaign began after the killing of her friend, Thomas Moss, in 1892. Moss owned a grocery store just outside Memphis and its success led to threats from white vigilantes, who resented the competition. One day, some plain-clothes police deputies descended on the store, and were shot and wounded by armed guards, in a case of mistaken identity. According to Moss's testimony and his wife's, he was at home at the time, but he and two employees, Calvin McDowell and William Stewart, were jailed, and held without bail for three days until a white mob dragged them off. In a barren field, they were shot, and McDowell's eyes were gouged out.

Wells was away at the time, and was horrified when she returned to Memphis. She wasn't the first person to write about lynching, but was the first to unpick the rape myth most often used to justify the violence. It was argued lynchings were necessary punishment for black men who raped white women – inherent in this was the idea that black men had a greater propensity to rape than white men. Wells exposed the fact that in many lynching cases there wasn't even a rape allegation, and when there was, there often existed a consensual relationship between a black man and a white woman – lynching was a way of terrorising the black community, and laying claim to white women's bodies. Proof of this last argument was the fact that the rape of black women was not punished by lynching, or generally at all.

Wells spent much of her career documenting the sexual assault of black women.

She wrote a series of editorials on lynching for *Free Speech* and a white mob descended on the newspaper's offices, destroying them, and leaving a note that anyone who published the paper 'would be punished with death'.

Wells left Memphis with a pistol in her purse, writes Bay, travelling to New York, and then the UK, where her supporters, including the Duke of Argyll, set up the British Anti-Lynching Committee. This didn't make Wells popular at home. *The New York Times* described her as 'a slanderous and nasty-minded mulattress'.

Wells kept going despite the backlash, writing the pamphlets *Southern Horrors* (1892) and *The Red Record* (1895). She married attorney Ferdinand Barnett in 1895, keeping her own name (she was known thereafter as Ida Wells-Barnett), and the couple had four children. She also became owner and editor of *The Conservator* newspaper.

Wells was involved in the formation of many influential groups, including the National Association for the Advancement of Colored People (NAACP), but was often sidelined – she refused to be deferential. Settling in Chicago, she set up the Negro Fellowship League to help young men who were struggling to survive, and too often criminalised. From the moment she refused to give up her seat, Wells spent a lifetime fighting for the good.

Shirin Ebadi

Lawyer, b.1947

Shirin Ebadi in Milan, May 2016.

'I am against patriarchy, not Islam'

In her 2016 memoir, *Until We Are Free*, Shirin Ebadi writes that being crushed 'simply gives you greater exercise in collecting the shards of yourself, putting them back together, and figuring out what to do next'.

That attitude has been essential, since attempts to crush Ebadi have been determined and legion. As a lawyer and defender of human rights in Iran, she has been imprisoned, as has her former husband and her sister. She has faced intense and longstanding surveillance and intimidation, and has had her house attacked by a mob shouting 'Death to the traitor Ebadi!'

In fact, such is the opposition to her work, that her 2006 and 2016 memoirs both begin with death threats. In *Iran Awakening* (2006), she writes about one chilling moment, when she was working on a case involving the premeditated killings of dozens of intellectuals in the late 1990s. The government had recently admitted partial complicity in these deaths, she writes. Reading the transcript of a conversation between a government minister and one of the people implicated in the killings, she came to the line: 'The next person to be killed is Shirin Ebadi'. Her would-be assassin had gone to the minister of intelligence 'requesting permission to execute my killing,' she continues. 'Not during the fasting month of Ramadan, the minister had replied, but anytime thereafter.'

The first chapter of *Until We Are Free* is bluntly titled 'Death Threat', and ends with a message tacked to her front door: 'If you go on as you are now, we will be forced to end your life. If you value it, stop slandering the Islamic Republic. Stop all this noise you are making outside the country. Killing you is the easiest thing we could do.'

Ebadi was born into a prosperous family – her father served as the country's deputy minister of agriculture – and she and her brother Jafar were treated equally by her parents, instilling a strong sense of gender parity. In 1953, the overthrow of Iran's democratically elected Prime Minister, Mohammad Mosaddegh, in a coup supported by the CIA and British intelligence services, led to her father being demoted to a much lower position. 'The coup convinced many Iranians that politics was dirty,' Ebadi writes, 'an intricate game of backroom deals and cloaked interests in which ordinary people were pawns.'

At Tehran University, she studied law, and found she was a natural activist; this was the mid-1960s, and there were plenty of protests on campus to attend. She decided to become a judge, achieving her ambition with impressive speed, in March 1970, aged 23. Five years later, she married electrical engineer, Javad Tavassolian, and a successful career and family life seemed assured.

The easy progress came to an end in 1979, as Iranians raised their voices against the ruling shah, calling for the cleric Ayatollah Khomeini to be their leader. At first, Ebadi was enthusiastic about the Iranian Revolution. 'Who did I have more in common with, in the end,' she writes, 'an opposition led by mullahs who spoke in the tones familiar to ordinary Iranians or the gilded court of the shah, whose officials cavorted with American starlets at parties soaked in expensive French champagne?' She joined those who took to the rooftops in Tehran, chanting Allahu Akbar.

Within months, she realised she'd made a mistake: 'I was a woman, and this revolution's victory demanded my defeat'. Soon, she was stripped of her judgeship, and ordered to be secretary of the court she had once presided over. 'I am against patriarchy, not Islam,' she has said, and from the day she lost her livelihood, she has repeated one refrain: 'an interpretation of Islam that is in harmony with equality and democracy is an authentic expression of faith,' she writes. 'It is not religion that binds women, but the selective dictates of those who wish them cloistered. That belief, along with the conviction that change in Iran must come peacefully and from within, has underpinned my work.'

Ebadi's daughter Negar was born in 1980, and Nargess in 1983. When women were allowed to practice law again in Iran, in 1992, she began working pro bono, using cases to highlight legal inequalities. The case of Leila Fathi, for instance, an eleven-year-old girl who had been raped and murdered by a group of three men, one of whom hanged himself in prison. Under the Islamic penal code in Iran, a man's life was worth twice a woman's life, and 'the judge ruled that the "blood money" for the two men was worth more than the life of the murdered eleven-year-old girl . . .' she writes. 'He demanded that her family come up with thousands of dollars to finance their executions.' Ebadi used the proceedings to draw attention to this biting inequality, writing an article for a magazine which high-lighted the fact that damage to a man's testicles was valued as equal to a woman's life. Unsurprisingly, this comparison piqued public interest.

In 2000, she was imprisoned for three weeks, at Evin Prison, and kept in solitary confinement, and in 2001 she co-founded the Defenders of Human Rights Centre, writing regular reports about human rights in Iran. When she won the Nobel Peace Prize in 2003, while on a trip to Paris, she was greeted by thousands of people, mainly women, on arriving back in Iran.

Ebadi has been accused, on many occasions, of being in league with the US, not least when the mob who attacked her house painted 'America Crone' on the wall. But she has consistently spoken out against western intervention in Iran and more broadly, insisting on Iranian self-determination.

Since 2009, following years of threats and intimidation, Ebadi has lived in exile from Iran. Even once she left the country, her family continued to be targeted: her sister was jailed for three weeks, and Javad was imprisoned too, lashed, and forced to denounce her on camera. Their marriage eventually buckled under the strain. But she has continued working, writing and speaking on behalf of human rights in Iran and beyond. 'The Iranian revolution has produced its own opposition,' she once wrote, 'not least a nation of educated, conscious women who are agitating for their rights.' She has been a mother of that fight.

Mary Wollstonecraft

Writer, 1759–1797

Mary Wollstonecraft by John Opie, c. 1797.

I n 1787, as she finished her first novel, Mary Wollstonecraft
wrote to her younger sisters that she was 'the first of a
new genus', a woman who made her living by writing.
Wollstonecraft was in her late twenties, living alone in south
London, part of a group of writers and artists who
congregated around publisher Joseph Johnson. She would
be a truly modern woman, in an age when women's
liberation seemed close to impossible.

Women were not properly educated, if at all, reliant on a
husband to survive. As Charlotte Gordon writes in *Romantic
Outlaws*, her biography of Wollstonecraft and her daughter
Mary Shelley, in this era, 'husbands had absolute power in
marriage. A wife was not allowed to own anything. She had
no legal rights of any kind . . . Husbands could beat their
wives and declare them insane. If a woman tried to flee, her
husband had the right to bring her back by force'. Divorce
was almost unheard of – during the eighteenth century,
notes Gordon, only four women won a legal separation –
and a 1782 reform suggested how long it would be until
spousal abuse was outlawed. This ruled that the stick a man

used to beat his wife must simply no longer be thicker than a thumb.

Wollstonecraft had seen the worst of marriage, growing up with her parents Edward and Elizabeth. The second of their seven children, she listened as her father, an alcoholic, raped and beat her mother; as a teenager, Wollstonecraft would stay up late to block her father's path to the parental bedroom. By age fifteen, she was close to a breakdown. She was saved by a couple called the Clares. Reverend Henry Clare introduced her to the works of John Locke, whose thoughts on equality were formative for Wollstonecraft.

Her view of marriage was influenced by other experiences too. When she was 24 she was called to help her younger sister Eliza, who was apparently suffering severe postnatal depression after having a baby a year into her marriage. As Eliza became more coherent, Wollstonecraft inferred that, in fact, she was afraid of her husband, who had been forcing himself on her. There was no law against rape within marriage in Britain until 1991, and Wollstonecraft spirited Eliza to a lodging house in Hackney, leaving behind her daughter, who was technically her husband's property. Saved from an impossible situation, Eliza was now in an extremely difficult one: unable to divorce and therefore unable to remarry, with no chance of employment if her flight became public.

Wollstonecraft decided to set up a school, providing employment for Eliza, their sister Everina, and her own close friend Fanny Blood. She had long wanted to set up a household with Fanny, who had been supporting her family since her late teens with her botanical sketches. In 1784, the school opened in Newington Green, which was then a village just outside London, and Wollstonecraft devised a progressive education for the pupils, most of whom were girls.

By Spring 1786, Blood had married, given birth, and died soon after; the school had failed; and Wollstonecraft decided to start writing. Joseph Johnson paid her £10 to publish *Thoughts on the Education of Daughters* (1787), and pledged future support too. Women had established themselves as writers before, including Mary Astell, Catherine Macaulay and Fanny Burney, but as Gordon writes, 'Mary was the first female writer who would receive a reliable stream of work from her publisher on a retainer basis'.

She became a book reviewer and translator, and when Edmund Burke wrote his conservative response to the revolution sweeping Paris, she wrote a rebuttal: *A Vindication of the Rights of Men* (1790). Published anonymously at first, it was received positively until her identity was revealed; writer Horace Walpole then called her a 'hyena in petticoats'. In 1792, she published her most enduringly influential work, *A Vindication of the Rights of Woman*, one of the great foundational feminist texts, in which she argued for women's education and liberty. 'My own sex, I hope, will excuse me, if I treat them like rational creatures, instead of flattering their *fascinating* graces, and viewing them as if they were in a state of perpetual childhood, unable to stand alone . . .' she wrote. 'I wish to persuade women to endeavour to acquire strength, both of mind and body.'

In December 1792, she travelled to Paris as a foreign correspondent, writing *An Historical and Moral View of the Origin and Progress of the French Revolution and the Effect it has Produced in Europe* (1794), including reflections on capitalism that remain relevant today. In reference to the 'destructive influence of commerce', for instance, she wrote that, as the industrial age developed, 'thus are whole knots of men turned into machines, to enable a keen speculator to become wealthy'.

In France she had a romance with US adventurer, and possible spy, Gilbert Imlay; her first child Fanny Imlay was born outside marriage when Wollstonecraft was 35. Back in London, Imlay seemed increasingly distant, and Wollstonecraft twice tried to kill herself, first with laudanum, then by jumping into the River Thames. Between these attempts, she went to Scandinavia, Fanny in tow, and the resulting book, *Letters Written During a Short Residence in Sweden, Norway, and Denmark* (1796), proved her biggest commercial success in her lifetime.

One of its most enthusiastic readers was political philosopher William Godwin. The pair began a relationship, and when Wollstonecraft became pregnant with her second daughter, she and Godwin decided to marry – despite their shared reservations about the institution – agreeing they would respect each other's independence and right to work.

Wollstonecraft died of septicaemia, eleven days after her daughter was born; Mary Godwin would go on to write the visionary novel, *Frankenstein*. In the months after his wife's death, William Godwin published an ill-considered memoir which ruined her reputation for the next two centuries, undermining her intellectual achievements while emphasising her sexual adventures. Not only was she damned as 'a whore' by critics, but any woman minded to follow her path knew she risked the same response.

'Every day she made theories by which life should be lived,' wrote Virginia Woolf of Wollstonecraft, 'and every day she came smack against the rock of other peoples' prejudices.' But she persisted, dauntless, determined to forge her own independence – and that of all women.

Frida Kahlo

Artist, 1907–1954

Frida Kahlo, c. 1950.

> *'I paint myself because I am so often alone, because I am the subject I know best'*

Frida Kahlo's art was born in suffering, as her paintings attest. Her famous 1944 work *The Broken Column* shows Kahlo naked, inside a surgical corset, flesh torn from chin to navel to expose a crumbling Ionic column where her spine should be, an image both monumental and intimate. Nails pierce her flesh; her eyes weep heavy tears. But it was Kahlo's commitment to life that made her work universal.

As a painter, she had a distinctively female perspective. Her husband, acclaimed Mexican muralist Diego Rivera, once wrote that after a particularly brutal miscarriage she began work on an unprecedented series of masterpieces, 'paintings which exalted the feminine qualities of endurance of truth, reality, cruelty, and suffering. Never before had a woman put such agonised poetry on canvas'.

The first of these paintings was *Henry Ford Hospital* (1932), which shows Kahlo nude in bed, the sheets below her waist covered in blood, red veins snaking from her hands, joining her umbilically to floating symbols including a foetus, a snail and an orchid. That same year she painted *My Birth*; this shows a woman, her body covered by a sheet from the waist up, with a large baby's head emerging from her vagina. The public was used to seeing female nudes arranged artfully for the male gaze, and in response to Kahlo's first one-woman exhibition, in New York, in 1938, an art critic sniffed that her work was 'more obstetrical than aesthetic'. But for many women, her images capture some of the essential qualities of life in a female body – the pleasures, pain and at once astonishing and terrifying reproductive possibilities. Surrealist André Breton once remarked that her art is 'a ribbon around a bomb'.

'The one who gave birth to herself . . . who wrote the most wonderful poem of her life,' wrote Kahlo in her diary, a tribute to her own acts of self-creation. She always insisted she had been born in 1910 – coming to flaming life at the start of the Mexican revolution – but was actually born in 1907, to a German photographer, Guillermo, who had emigrated to Mexico and married her pious mother Matilde.

Aged six, Kahlo contracted polio, spending nine months confined to her room. The illness left her right leg withered, and her father encouraged her to take up sports including boxing, wrestling and football, unusual activities for a Mexican girl of that era.

At the National Preparatory School, reputedly the best school in the country, she met her first serious boyfriend, Alejandro Gómez Arias, and on 17 September 1925, she had the accident which would shape her life and inspire her first paintings.

She and Arias were on a bus when a streetcar collided with it. An iron rod, 'went through Frida from one side to the other at the level of the pelvis . . .' Arias told Kahlo's biographer Hayden Herrera. 'Something strange had happened. Frida was totally nude. The collision had unfastened her clothes. Someone in the bus, probably a house painter, had been carrying a packet of powdered gold. This package broke, and the gold fell all over the bleeding body of Frida. When people saw her they cried, "La bailarina, la bailarina!" With the gold on her red, bloody body, they thought she was a dancer.'

Her spinal column, collarbone, third and fourth ribs, right leg, right foot and pelvis were broken, and her left shoulder was dislocated; the doctors assumed she would die on the operating table. Instead, she had the first of 32 surgeries over the course of her life.

The next year, she painted a self-portrait for Arias, and in 1928, after the couple had broken up, Kahlo started showing her paintings to friends. She had met Rivera casually a few years earlier, when he was painting a mural at her school; at the time she had announced, much to her school friends' astonishment, that one day she would have his child. Now she visited him and asked for his professional verdict. He told her she had talent, and years later wrote that, in that one encounter, 'Frida had already become the most important fact in my life'. On 21 August 1929, they were married.

Their turbulent relationship was marked by affairs – he most notably with her sister Cristina, she with Marxist revolutionary Leon Trotsky. Kahlo also had relationships with women, and once told a friend her attitude to life was 'make love, take a bath, make love again'.

Rivera was among the most famous painters in the world, and Kahlo existed in his shadow; when the couple were living in the US and *The Detroit News* interviewed her, they described her as a 'dabbler'. In 1939, the couple divorced, and Kahlo, determined to support herself financially, entered her most disciplined period, producing more work than she had throughout her marriage. But the pair soon reconciled, remarrying in 1940.

Kahlo's later years were among her most difficult, physically, culminating in the amputation of her gangrenous right leg in August 1953. She took to drinking a bottle of brandy a day, and when a doctor friend advised her to abstain from alcohol, developed a dependency on the painkiller Demerol.

But her commitment to life continued. Her passions were painting, Rivera, communism and the love of Mexican history and heritage that defines her work. When the Galeria Arte Contemporaneo in Mexico City organised an exhibition of her paintings in 1953, she was brought to the opening on a stretcher, holding court from a bed at the heart of the gallery.

'I hope the exit is joyful – and I hope never to come back – Frida,' were the final words in her diary, leading to suspicions she had killed herself, although the cause of death was reportedly a pulmonary embolism. Eight days before her death she completed a still-life of watermelons, one slice inscribed with her tribute to a life lived fully: 'Viva la Vida'. In the crematorium, Herrera writes, as her body moved towards the furnace, the heat caused her corpse to sit up suddenly, hair alight, with a hint of a smile. Shocking for the mourners, but perfectly dramatic to the last.

Rosalind Franklin

Scientist, 1920–1958

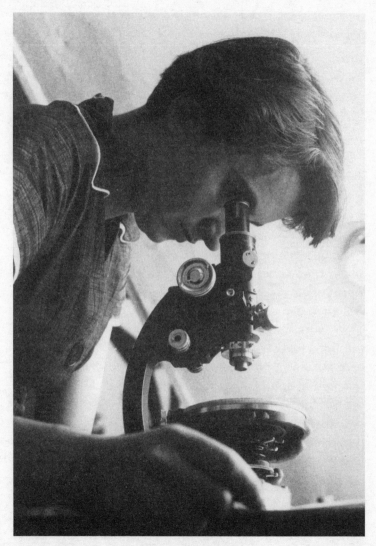

Rosalind Franklin, 1955.

*'Science and everyday
life cannot and should
not be separated'*

In May 1952, a photograph was taken that unlocked the secret of life. Rosalind Franklin was unhappily employed at King's College London, at loggerheads with her colleague Maurice Wilkins, but absorbed in her work on DNA fibres, which she and PhD student Raymond Gosling were photographing at close range, with a specially designed camera, each exposure lasting up to 100 hours. Their work had already prompted one significant break-through, revealing that there were two forms of DNA fibres, A and B, the first short and dry, the second long, thin and hydrated. Photograph 51 was the clearest image yet of the B fibre, and in these days just before the structure of deoxyribonucleic acid was discovered, the dynamic criss-cross pattern was a revelation. As Brenda Maddox writes in her biography of Franklin, *The Dark Lady of DNA* (2002), the photograph unquestionably showed a helix.

Franklin numbered the photo, and set it aside. She was a meticulous experimentalist who didn't believe in making models until the data was complete, her work always based on evidence rather than intuition.

James Watson had a different approach. A US scientist, then in his early twenties, he was working with British colleague Francis Crick at the Cavendish Laboratory in Cambridge, and was determined to win the race to discover the structure of DNA. Word arrived from the US towards the end of 1952 that Linus Pauling, the era's leading chemist, had made the breakthrough, and Watson was devastated. But Pauling's paper, which arrived in the UK in late January 1953, included a fatal error, writes Maddox. 'What he was proposing as a structure for nucleic acid was not an acid at all'.

There was now a small window of opportunity; Watson estimated it at six weeks. A couple of days after Pauling's paper arrived, Watson walked into Franklin's office unannounced, without knocking, and implied, 'she was incompetent in interpreting X-ray pictures,' he writes in his book *The Double Helix*. He had heard from Wilkins that Franklin was 'definitely anti-helical' – that she didn't believe DNA formed a helix – which was not true. 'Suddenly Rosy came from behind the lab bench that separated us and began moving towards me,' writes Watson. 'Fearing that in her hot anger she might strike me, I grabbed up the Pauling manuscript and hastily retreated to the open door.'

Franklin died of ovarian cancer, aged 37, and the first glimpse the general public had of her was in Watson's bestselling book, published in 1968, a decade after her death. It was not a flattering portrait. Throughout, Watson called her by the diminutive Rosy, and his observations include the comment that, 'she might have been quite stunning had she taken even a mild interest in clothes'.

On Franklin's difficult relationship with Wilkins, Watson wrote that 'clearly Rosy had to go or be put in her place' and 'the best home for a feminist was in another person's lab'.

It has been suggested that the nature of Watson's portrait of Franklin perhaps related to the circumstances in which he made use of her work in his discovery – work he had been shown without her knowledge.

It was on 30 January 1953 that Wilkins showed Photograph 51 to Watson, who wrote later that as soon as he saw it, 'my mouth fell open and my pulse began to race'. By the end of the day, he had decided DNA's structure must be a double helix; within a week he and Crick had begun building their model; and on 28 February 1953, writes Watson, Crick arrived at their local pub, 'and told everybody he had found the secret of life'. The final model was completed on 7 March, and a paper published in *Nature* soon afterwards.

In 1962, Wilkins, Watson and Crick won the Nobel Prize; Wilkins was the only one to mention Franklin in his speech. Decades later, Watson and Crick would acknowledge that her work had been critical to their breakthrough.

'All her life Rosalind knew exactly where she was going,' her mother once said, 'and at the age of sixteen, she took science for her subject'. Born into a wealthy family, she studied Natural Sciences at Cambridge, before a PhD in physical chemistry. She believed in arguing the point, equipped with the facts; 'confrontation when cornered was Rosalind's tactic' writes Maddox. Determined as a child, she was indefatigable as an adult. In her final years, afflicted with the tumours some have speculated resulted from her work with radiation, she kept going. 'She would crawl up the narrow stairs from where the X-ray apparatus was, to her office on the first floor,' Maddox notes, 'refusing all offers to be carried.'

For all her toughness and tenacity, she was clearly a good friend, warm, generous and happy in the company of her small nieces and nephews. It was her friend Anne Sayre who began the process of rescuing Franklin's reputation in 1975, with her book *Rosalind Franklin and DNA*, a riposte to Watson.

Franklin was a much appreciated mentor to scientists including Aaron Klug, with whom she collaborated at Birkbeck College on the study of viruses – a contented workplace, following her unhappy time at King's. Klug won the Nobel Prize in 1982, and said on receiving it that had Franklin's life 'not been cut tragically short, she might well have stood in this place on an earlier occasion'.

Nobel prizes aren't awarded posthumously, and each single prize is given to at most three people, but it has been suggested Franklin would have had a strong claim to be included in the 1962 chemistry award, had she survived. Beyond the prizes she never chased, the tragedy is that Franklin lost the chance to pursue her genius. She was a scientist, wrote J. D. Bernal, who employed her at Birkbeck, 'distinguished by extreme clarity and perfection in everything she undertook'. What else might she have discovered, given time?

Wangari Maathai

Environmentalist, 1940–2011

Wangari Maathai.

> *'Each person needs to raise their consciousness to a certain level so that they will not give up or succumb'*

Fearlessness is really persistence, writes Wangari Maathai in her autobiography, *Unbowed*. 'Because I am focused on the solution, I don't see danger'. She needed boundless courage in a lifetime campaigning for the environment, democracy and peace, during which she was imprisoned, beaten, forced into hiding, and feared for her life.

Born in Kenya in 1940, when the country was under British rule, she had a rural childhood. Her mother gave her a small garden, where she planted beans, maize and millet; elephants, monkeys and leopards lived in the nearby forest. One of the few Kenyan girls of that era to graduate high school, Maathai went on to study in the US, part of a programme led by figures including then senator John F. Kennedy, which became known as the Kennedy Airlift.

Returning to Kenya with an MA in biology as well as her undergraduate degree, she went to work in the Department of Veterinary Anatomy at the University College of Nairobi, and registered for a PhD. In 1971, she became the first woman in East and Central Africa to be awarded a doctorate.

By this time she was married to an aspiring politician called Mwangi Mathai, with whom she would have three children. She was appointed senior lecturer in the School of Veterinary Medicine; she and her colleague Vertistine Mbaya were the first African women employed in the department. They realised they were being denied the enefits of their male colleagues – including holiday pay and housing – and fought for equality. Other women were urged to join their campaign, but many refused, and Maathai's eyes opened to entrenched and unchallenged gender discrimination.

In the 1970s she became aware of the problem of soil erosion; landslides were becoming more common, clean drinking water was increasingly scarce and malnutrition was rising. The answer struck her during the first UN conference on women in Mexico City in 1975. They should plant trees. These would 'provide a supply of wood that would enable women to cook nutritious foods . . .' she writes. 'The trees would offer shade for humans and animals, protect watersheds and bind the soil.'

Her Green Belt Movement was born in 1977. The global women's movement was thriving and the programme was designed to empower Kenyan women, who were paid a stipend for each tree they planted. In its first four decades, more than 50 million trees were planted in Kenya, and the movement inspired the UN's billion tree campaign, which began in 2006. More than 12 billion trees were planted worldwide in its first five years.

Maathai's husband filed for divorce in 1979, accusing her of adultery and cruelty. She denied this, and the case went to court; after she posed a question from the stand to her husband's lawyer, he turned to the judge: 'If she dares ask me a question in court,' he said, 'what do you think she does to my client at home?' Maathai knew the case was lost. Mwangi had been quoted as saying he wanted a divorce because she was 'too educated, too strong, too successful, too stubborn, and too hard to control'. She didn't remember him saying this in court, but it was perhaps a summation of how the press perceived her.

In an interview not long afterwards, Maathai suggested the divorce judge must have been either incompetent or corrupt, and she was charged with contempt of court, and sentenced to six months in jail. After three days, she was freed, but her legal problems had begun – the result, she suspected, of challenging male authority.

Kenya gained independence in 1963, and over time, writes Maathai, it became a de facto one-party state. In 1988, the Green Belt Movement joined other groups in pushing for greater political freedom, and the next year Maathai also challenged the government decision to build a skyscraper in Uhuru Park in Nairobi, which would encroach significantly on public space. President Daniel arap Moi suggested if she was a proper African woman she would keep quiet. Nonetheless, the campaign succeeded, and this, Maathai believed, marked 'the beginning of the end of Kenya as a one-party state'. She had taken on the authorities and won, giving other people the confidence to speak out.

In early 1992, amid rumours the government planned to hand power to the army, she heard she was on a list of people targeted for assassination. That same day, pro-democracy campaigners were arrested, and she barricaded herself in her home for three days, until the police sawed through the bars on her windows. Charged with treason, which carried the death penalty, she went to jail again, before being released on bail. In November 1992 all charges were dropped.

But she was still under threat. When ethnic tensions began brewing in the Rift Valley, Maathai and friends went to bear witness to the destruction, and the government claimed she was crusading for the supremacy of her tribal group, the Kikuyu. An MP threatened her with forcible circumcision if she returned to the valley, and she began to genuinely fear for her life. She went into hiding, moving between safe houses.

It was as she planted a tree in Karura Forest in the late 1990s, in protest at swathes of the land being given to developers and government allies, that she came closest to losing her life. The campaigners were confronted by guards, and Maathai was left with a serious head wound. She signed the formal complaint of assault with an X, in her own blood.

In 2002, Kenya had a free and fair election, and Maathai ran, winning 98 per cent of the votes in her Tetu constituency. In the new government she became assistant environmental minister.

She campaigned against the debts poor countries had to pay richer ones, and in 2004 was awarded the Nobel Peace Prize. Maathai proved it was possible – with great persistence, against great opposition – to create something extraordinary: to plant a forest that spanned the world.

Louise Bourgeois

Artist, 1911–2010

Louise Bourgeois posing with one of her marble sculptures, *Sleep II*, at the Museum of Modern Art, New York, February 1983.

In 1988, the Guerrilla Girls, a group of anonymous women artists, published an advertisement in the magazine *Artforum*. 'The Advantages of Being a Woman Artist' was the title of a sarcastic list of benefits that included working without the pressure of success; seeing your ideas live on in the work of others; and not having to undergo the embarrassment of being called a genius. Also, 'Knowing your career might pick up after you're eighty'.

Louise Bourgeois didn't have to wait quite that long for recognition – it was in her seventies that she became world famous. Deborah Wye, a young curator, encouraged the Museum of Modern Art in New York to give her a retrospective, and in 1982 Bourgeois's vision, soft and violent by turns, reached the public consciousness, as did the story she told to explain it. In an autobiographical photo essay, she described her early life, during which her domineering father Louis had an affair with the young English governess who lived with the family. This betrayal continued for ten years, tolerated by her mother Josephine.

This story has been used to read much of Bourgeois's work, before and since, including her 1974 sculpture,

The Destruction of the Father – a table surrounded by large breast-like protuberances, on which is arrayed what appear to be hunks of meat. This was, said Bourgeois, a scene in which a father's children have killed and eaten him. The implied violence continues in her 1990–93 work *Cell (Choisy)*, in which a pink marble replica of her childhood home is displayed in a wire cage, beneath a suspended guillotine blade. 'Every day you have to abandon your past or accept it,' Bourgeois wrote in her photo essay, 'and then if you cannot accept it you become a sculptor.'

Born on the Left Bank of Paris on Christmas Day 1911, she and her family moved to Choisy-le-Roi a few years later, where her parents ran a successful tapestry restoration business. Bourgeois remembered her mother clipping out genitalia in the tapestries (some buyers were particularly chaste), while the young artist helped by drawing missing feet or horses' hooves.

She was close to her mother, who had suffered Spanish flu in the outbreak after the First World War; in the late 1990s, Bourgeois created a sculpture, entitled *Maman*, a spindly legged spider, more than 30 feet tall, which has stalked some of the world's best art galleries, from the Tate Modern in London, to the Guggenheim in Bilbao. 'The Spider is an ode to my mother,' Bourgeois said. 'She was my best friend'.

As a child, Bourgeois loved mathematics, and went to the Sorbonne to study geometry, but abandoned this when her mother died in 1932. She threw herself into a river a few days afterwards; her father pulled her out. From then on, she committed herself to art, supporting herself as best she could, and studying with various teachers, including

Fernand Léger, who informed her, perceptively, that she was a sculptor rather than a painter.

In the 1930s she opened a print shop, and there she met her husband, US art historian, Robert Goldwater. He bought some Picasso prints and 'in between talks about Surrealism and the latest trends,' she said later, 'we got married'. The couple moved to New York, adopted a son, and Bourgeois gave birth to two more boys.

From 1945–55 she made sculptures known as *Personages*, tall, thin structures, with a nod to figuration and Giacometti. These were carved in balsa wood, which didn't produce much noise or mess – she could work without disturbing her young family. Bourgeois had her first solo show in 1945, but after her father's death in 1951, she stopped showing new work for eleven years, and entered psychoanalysis. She has described psychological struggles which included up to four anxiety attacks a day, and insomnia continuing over four nights. The psychoanalysis lasted more than 30 years.

Bourgeois wasn't showing her work, but she was still making it. The 1950s were macho, she once said, and 'the fact that the market was not interested in my work because I was a woman was a blessing in disguise. It allowed me to work totally undisturbed'. This seclusion ended in 1966, when curator Lucy Lippard included Bourgeois's work in her influential show *Eccentric Abstraction*. Feminist art was flowering. In 1970, Judy Chicago set up her Feminist Art Program at what is now California State University; in 1971, art historian Linda Nochlin published the groundbreaking essay, 'Why Have There Been No Great Women Artists?'; that same year, the *Where We At* exhibition of black women artists in New York led to a collective of the same name; and in 1976, Nochlin and art historian Ann Sutherland Harris curated *Women Artists: 1550–1950*, introducing artists including Artemisia Gentileschi and Angelica Kauffmann to a much wider audience.

In 1973, Bourgeois was widowed, and her work blossomed. She was ambivalent about feminism, exploring ideas and emotions in her art which she considered pre-gender. Not aligned with any specific movement, the word most often used to define her in her later years was indefatigable. 'A woman has no peace as an artist until she proves over and over that she won't be eliminated,' she said, and she was still working six days a week in her nineties, holding artist salons at her home on the seventh day, creating the work that, in the words of her long-time assistant Jerry Gorovy, made women the subject of art, rather than the object. Frances Morris, who curated a 2007 Bourgeois retrospective at Tate Modern, described her as 'a lone female innovator hacking through the undergrowth of New York's macho urban jungle', while art critic Adrian Searle wrote: 'entire careers could be made from tiny ideas she has used briefly then discarded. She could have had twenty careers'. Recognition may have come late, but it was fulsome and sure.

Wilma Rudolph

Olympic athlete, 1940–1994

Wilma Rudolph at the Summer Olympic Games in Rome, Italy in 1960.

*'Believe me, the reward
is not so great without
the struggle'*

Wilma Rudolph made it look so easy. At the 1960 Olympics in Rome, she strolled across the finish line in the 100 metre and 200 metre races, strides ahead of her competitors, before running the final leg of the 4 x 100 metre relay to another victory, the first American woman to win three gold medals at one Olympic Games. These were the first Olympics ever televised in the US, and it was also the first time most Americans had seen women compete on screen. Olympic historian Bud Greenspan compared Rudolph's achievement to that of Jesse Owens, the African-American athlete whose performance at the 1936 Olympics made a mockery of Adolf Hitler's belief in Aryan supremacy. 'Like Jesse,' said Greenspan, 'she changed the sport for all time. She became the benchmark for little black girls to aspire to.'

Born prematurely, weighing 4.5 pounds, Rudolph was the twentieth of her father Ed's 22 children. Ed was a railway porter, and her mother Blanche, his second wife, was a domestic worker for white families in their segregated community. As described in Maureen M Smith's biography of Rudolph, the runner grew up in Clarksville, Tennessee, with no electricity, wearing dresses made from flour sacks.

By age seven, Rudolph had suffered double pneumonia, scarlet fever, mumps, measles and whooping cough; she had also contracted polio, aged four, which paralysed her left leg. She started wearing a steel brace, travelling with her mother to a hospital 50 miles away, because the local one wouldn't treat black patients.

Her mother and siblings began massaging her leg four times a day. 'My doctor told me I would never walk again,' she wrote later. 'My mother told me I would. I believed my mother.' At six she began to hop, at eight she could walk with a leg brace, and at nine she walked into church without it. When she was eleven, all walking aids were abandoned.

Rudolph was soon on the basketball team at junior high, twice made the all-state team, and set a state record, scoring 49 points in one match. Ed Temple, who coached the women's track and field programme at Tennessee State University, invited her to his summer school, and at sixteen, Rudolph – the girl who was told she would never walk – qualified for the 1956 Olympics in Melbourne. She won a bronze medal for the 4 x 100 metre relay.

When the modern Olympics began in Athens in 1896, all 245 competitors were men; the founder of the International Olympic Committee, Pierre de Coubertin, felt women competitors would be 'impractical, uninteresting, unaesthetic'. Over the years, women were gradually allowed to compete, but progress wasn't constant. In 1928, for instance, when six women collapsed following the 800 metre race, it was discontinued, and from then until 1960, the longest race for women at the Olympics was the 200 metres. Sport might damage a woman's health and reproductive capabilities it was thought, and to be strong and muscular was considered unfeminine. Temple, an outstanding champion of women athletes, nonetheless had a motto: 'I don't want oxes, I want foxes'.

After the 1956 Olympics, Rudolph became pregnant with her first child Yolanda, by her high school sweetheart Robert Eldridge. Temple had a rule against mothers joining his university team, the Tigerbelles, but he waived this and Yolanda went to live with Rudolph's family. Rudolph began her degree in elementary education, on a scholarship requiring her to work on campus; at Tennessee State, a black university, resources were stretched thin. Ed Temple headed the US women's track and field team at the Rome Olympics that year, while also coaching the Tigerbelles, conducting two sociology classes six times a week and running the university post office. Rudolph and her teammates drew the lines on the running track themselves.

During a stopover in Hawaii on the way to the Melbourne Olympics, a white woman shouted at Rudolph and her teammates, 'what are you natives doing out in the street?' and a bus driver once refused to drive her integrated team to an athletics meet. In Rudolph's home state, Tennessee, that year, hundreds of African-American students were campaigning against segregation, enduring beatings and arrests during protests which involved them sitting calmly at lunch counters, asking to be served. In April 1960, the home of the students' lawyer was bombed. No one was hurt, but the dangers were clear.

Rudolph qualified for the 1960 games amid this tumult, and her prospects were good until the day before the heats, when she sprained her ankle. She ran with it strapped in the finals, completing the 100 metre race in eleven seconds, the fastest time in the world to that date, but which couldn't be credited due to the strong following wind. She broke the

Olympic record in the 200 metre race, and the world record in the relay.

A parade was prepared to welcome Rudolph home to Clarksville, and she said she wouldn't participate if it was segregated. It became the first integrated event in the town's history.

Rudolph gave up racing in 1962. Athletics was strictly amateur at the time, she couldn't earn a living from the sport and decided to go out as the fastest woman in the world. She graduated, married Eldridge and had three more children. Over the years, she struggled to find good, secure employment – though there were periods of teaching and coaching. 'People always thought of Wilma Rudolph as a threat,' she said in the early 1980s. 'In college I was an education major and qualified for several jobs. But the fame that came with the Olympic medals was too threatening to many people. Being a woman, being black and being Wilma Rudolph worked against me.'

In 1994, aged 54, Rudolph died as a result of a malignant brain tumour. Asked once how she compared to other runners, she abstained. 'I'm selfish,' she said. 'I think I was in a class all by myself.'

Virginia Woolf

Writer, 1882–1941

A portrait of Virginia Woolf taken by George C. Beresford, 1902.

> *'The balance between the outer and the inner is, after all, a terribly precarious business'*

How best to describe the way women's lives have been shrunk and circumscribed throughout history? In her classic 1929 essay 'A Room of One's Own', Virginia Woolf created the perfect character to express this: Shakespeare's Sister. This gifted sibling, she wrote, was left unschooled, unable to learn grammar and logic, and forced towards an early marriage: 'she cried out that marriage was hateful to her, and for that she was severely beaten by her father'. Not yet seventeen, she travelled to London to become an actor, and instead became pregnant. Her life ends, Woolf suggests, with death by her own hand. 'That, more or less, is how the story would run, I think, if a woman in Shakespeare's day had had Shakespeare's genius.'

Women had traditionally been deprived of the life of the mind; the kind of life, Woolf famously insisted, that required an income of £500 a year, and a room of one's own. Woolf's fiction took us into people's minds – those of men and women, but particularly women – showing that however confined by social and sexual convention, however small and domestic their life might look from the outside, their inner world could be epic. As part of a generation of modernists, including James Joyce and T. S. Eliot, writing through the world wars, she discarded the formalities of plot, and created instead a portrait of consciousness.

In her essay 'Modern Fiction', published in 1921, she describes the approach. 'Examine for a moment an ordinary mind on an ordinary day,' she writes. 'The mind receives a myriad impressions – trivial, fantastic, evanescent, or engraved with the sharpness of steel. From all sides they come, an incessant shower of innumerable atoms; and as they fall, as they shape themselves into the life of Monday or Tuesday, the accent falls differently from of old . . . Life is not a series of gig lamps, symmetrically arranged; life is a luminous halo, a semi-transparent envelope surrounding us from the beginning of consciousness to the end. Is it not the task of the novelist to convey this varying, this unknown and uncircumscribed spirit, whatever aberration or complexity it may display, with as little mixture of the alien and external as possible?'

Periods of breakdown punctuated Woolf's life, but she remained fiercely productive. As her biographer Hermione Lee writes, 'even in a year broken by illness (such as 1925) she would finish revising and publish one novel and a collection of essays, write eight or so short stories, start work on another novel, publish 37 review articles, keep a full diary, read a great number of books and write a great number of letters'. She was well-acquainted with many of the leading artists and writers of the day, as part of the Bloomsbury Group, which included her beloved older sister, the painter Vanessa Bell, as well as Lytton Strachey, John Maynard Keynes and E. M. Forster. In 1939, when she met Sigmund Freud, he gave her a narcissus.

The sweep of her life has led many, understandably, to reduce it to fragments. When researching Woolf's life, writes Lee, she was asked four questions again and again: 'Is it true that she was sexually abused as a child? What was her madness and why did she kill herself? Was Leonard a good or a wicked husband? Wasn't she the most terrible snob?' (To that final question, her diary entry on James Joyce's *Ulysses* is often produced as evidence for the prosecution: 'An illiterate, underbred book, it seems to me; the book of a self-taught working man, and we all know how distressing they are, how egotistic, insistent, raw, striking, and ultimately nauseating.')

She was born in 1882, into a family marked by death. Her parents, Leslie and Julia Stephen, had both lost their first spouse; they had four children between them when they married, and went on to have four more together, including Virginia. Julia had been a model for Pre-Raphaelite painters including Edward Burne-Jones, and posed too for her aunt, pioneering photographer Julia Margaret Cameron. Leslie Stephen was a writer, the first editor of *The Dictionary of National Biography*, and his first wife, Minny, was the daughter of novelist William Thackeray. As many as seventeen people lived in the family home, 22 Hyde Park Gate, at any one time.

Woolf was molested by her half-brother, Gerald Duckworth, when she was a small child, and although the details are less clear, she also seems to have been sexually abused by George Duckworth, the oldest of the siblings, in late adolescence. Her mother died when she was thirteen, the first of a series of deaths, followed by her half-sister Stella Duckworth two years later in 1897, her father in 1904, and her brother Thoby in 1906. The death of her mother, she said, was 'the greatest disaster that could happen', while her father's death provoked more complicated feelings. Had he lived another few decades, she wrote later, 'his life would have entirely ended mine . . . No writing, no books; – inconceivable'.

There was a breakdown after her mother's death, and an especially severe one after her father's death. 'Five times in her life,' writes Lee, '(four of them between the ages of thirteen and 33) she suffered from major onslaughts of the illness and in almost all (possibly all) of these attacks she attempted to kill herself.' It's been suggested she had bipolar disorder, and with psychiatry still in its infancy her treatment tended towards rest cures and sedatives.

Woolf started writing professionally in the early days of the twentieth century, and published her first two novels, *The Voyage Out* (1915) and *Night and Day* (1919), with the eponymous company created by Gerald Duckworth. She married Leonard Woolf in 1912, and five years later, they created the Hogarth Press, publishing her novel *Jacob's Room* in 1922, and an edition of T. S. Eliot's masterpiece *The Waste Land* in 1923. Her extraordinary run of experimental novels included *Mrs Dalloway* (1925), *To the Lighthouse* (1927) and *Orlando* (1928).

Woolf's death is, sadly, perhaps the best known part of her story. In March 1941, with stones in her pockets, she walked into the River Ouse. But if she experienced deep depression, she was also a sparkling conversationalist, full of life, witty, vital, brilliant. In the final letter she left for Leonard Woolf, she testifies to her happiness, however distant it must have seemed. 'If anybody could have saved me it would have been you,' she wrote. 'Everything has gone from me but the certainty of your goodness. I can't go on spoiling your life any longer. I don't think two people could have been happier than we have been.'

Martha Graham

Dancer, 1894–1991

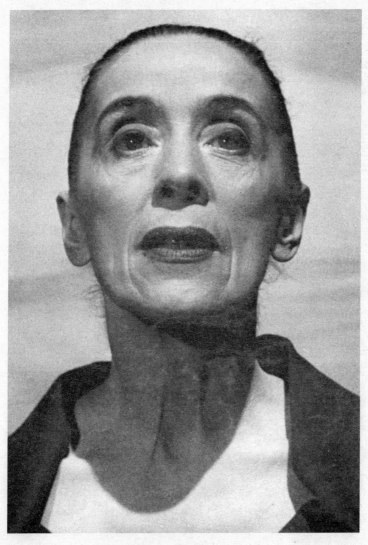

Martha Graham, c. 1965.

> *'I'd rather an audience like me than dislike me, but I'd rather they disliked me than be apathetic, because that is the kiss of death'*

On tour in a vaudeville revue in the early 1920s, Martha Graham visited the Art Institute of Chicago. This was the first time she had seen modern art, and in a room hung with Chagalls and Matisses, one work particularly struck her. 'I saw across the room a beautiful painting, what was then called abstract art, a startling new idea,' she wrote in her 1991 autobiography, *Blood Memory*. 'I nearly fainted because at that moment I knew I was not mad, that others saw the world, saw art, the way I did. It was by Wassily Kandinsky, and had a streak of red going from one end to the other. I said, "I will do that some day. I will make a dance like that".'

During a career lasting more than 70 years, Graham created around 180 original dances, her choreography radically reimagining how women are seen. John Martin, *The New York Times* dance critic from 1927–1962, wrote that 'no other dancer has yet touched the borders to which she has extended the compass of movement'.

Modern dance – or as Graham preferred to call it, contemporary dance – broke with the classical ballet tradition which dominated western dance between the sixteenth and nineteenth centuries. Dance critic Roger Copeland has written about the female stereotypes that emerged in this era, under the direction of male choreographers, the 'delicate, chaste women who die of unrequited love or romantic betrayal (*Giselle*), or who lay waiting to be awakened from their passive slumbers by a handsome prince (*Sleeping Beauty*) or mechanical dolls who (unlike Ibsen's *Nora*) remain confined within their doll's house (*Coppelia*)'. In contrast, the choreographers of modern dance were women, creating works for themselves, reflecting their own bodies and ideals. Isadora Duncan, for instance, moved away from the rigidity of ballet, and encouraged women to abandon their corsets.

Ruth St Denis was another pioneer, and on seeing her perform in Los Angeles in 1911 – the first time she had ever seen a dance performance – Graham decided 'I would dance, and when I learned she had a school I made up my mind to attend it'.

Five years later, aged 22, she went to study with St Denis and her husband Ted Shawn. Her prospects weren't good. On completing her audition, St Denis passed her to the care of Shawn (who was 'a dud' according to Graham); Shawn's recollection of her, decades later, was just as biting. 'She was quite a few years above the average age of all the other girls in the school,' he said. 'Let's admit that she was homely, and Martha was overweight. I won't say exactly fat, but she was dumpy, unprepossessing.'

She might be good enough, in time, to be a teacher, St Denis and Shawn concluded. Graham wasn't deterred. As she writes in *Blood Memory*, she didn't choose to be a dancer, 'I was chosen to be a dancer, and with that, you live all your life'. She would wake at night and practise until dawn – when another dancer was taken ill, she proved she was ready to dance the necessary solo.

She was tough and hot-tempered from the start. Shawn cast her as a princess in a dance he was choreographing; he played an emperor. In one scene, depicting an attempted rape, 'he grabbed me and dropped me on my head and I passed out for a few seconds,' wrote Graham. 'When I came to I bit him on his arm and drew blood . . . it became a great 'scandale' in the school. I suppose that is when my reputation for having a violent temper began. I was savage at that time. The critics said that onstage I blazed.'

She went on to the Greenwich Village Follies, leaving in 1925 to teach and work on her repertoire. A friend loaned her $1,000 to hire a Broadway theatre for a showcase, and the evening was a success, which Graham attributed partly to the curiosity value of seeing a woman perform her own work.

Between 1926 and 1930 she choreographed 79 new dances, including the short solo, *Revolt* (1927), described by Russell Freedman in his biography of Graham as her 'first dance of social protest, a stark, forceful comment on injustice'. These themes continued the next year, with the solo Immigrant, and the anti-war work *Poems of 1917.* In her autobiography Graham writes that many of the women who wanted to join her company 'came to me with conventional notions of prettiness and graceful posturing. I wanted them to admire strength. If I could give them only one thing, that would be it. Ugliness, I told them, if given a powerful voice, can be beautiful'.

Her choreography cast out the romance and fragility of ballet. She and her dancers performed barefoot, and her work was based on an understanding of breathing patterns, and often featured odd, unexpected angles. (Writer Stark Young once commented, pejoratively, 'she looks as though she were about to give birth to a cube'.) Her dancers referred to their training as 'the torture', and in an unexpected passage in her memoir, Graham writes that her school became known as 'the House of the Pelvic Truth' due to her advice that students needed to move from their vaginas.

In 1932, she became the first dancer ever to be given the prestigious Guggenheim Fellowship and in 1935 the Nazis asked her and her company to perform at the International Dance Festival, as part of the upcoming Berlin Olympics. She refused. The first man joined her troupe in 1938 – Erick Hawkins, with whom she would have a nine-year relationship – and she continued to create dances, including the 1943 *Deaths and Entrances*, which critic Anna Kisselgoff described as a 'modern psychological portrait of creative energy in women going to waste'.

Graham played a young bride opposite Hawkins in her classic work, *Appalachian Spring*, when she was 50; she had no intention of giving up dancing. After her final performance, in her mid-seventies, she fell into a black despair, drinking heavily. She had lost the will to live. 'Then, one morning,' she writes, 'I felt something well up within me. I knew that I would bloom again.' And she did. The last dance she choreographed premiered six months before she died, aged 96.

Zaha Hadid

Architect, 1950–2016

Zaha Hadid outside the Riverside Museum in Glasgow, June 2011.

'There are 360 degrees, so why stick to one?'

In the mid-1990s, controversy erupted over Zaha Hadid's design for a new opera house in Cardiff. Her proposals were derided as too modernist, mocked as a 'crystal necklace', and it was suggested they were so close in design to the shrine in Mecca that the city risked a fatwa. The plans had been chosen out of 269 designs. But before long, they were dropped.

The decision arguably illustrated the 'triple whammy' of prejudice Hadid sometimes spoke of. As she described it to BBC journalist Kirsty Young, 'I'm a woman, which is a problem to many people. I'm a foreigner – another big problem. And I do work which is not normative, which is not what they expect. So, together, it becomes difficult'. The decision also, ironically, represented the moment her career switched gear. Peter Palumbo, a member of the jury who had backed that design, told *The New Yorker* magazine that it, 'put the iron into her. She said, 'Right, I'm not going to let that happen again''.

Hadid had been known as a 'paper architect' for decades, famous for her designs but unable to get anything built. At the Architectural Association, where she studied in the

1970s, she had been a sensation, with her teacher and mentor, renowned Dutch architect Rem Koolhaas, writing that 'she is a PLANET in her own inimitable orbit. That status has its own rewards and difficulties: due to the flamboyance and intensity of her work, it will be impossible [for her] to have a conventional career.'

After graduating in 1977, Hadid worked on a new visual language, incorporating speed, movement, fluidity; she liked the idea of buildings that could float, she said. She established a practice in London in 1980, creating large abstract paintings to express her designs. These were exhibited to acclaim in the 1988 show Deconstructivist Architecture at New York's Museum of Modern Art.

Still, nothing was built.

She was visionary; a digital architect before the technology existed. But as digital tools developed, her visions became reality. The first major building was a fire station in Germany, completed in 1993, a shard of concrete jutting into the sky. In 2005, her design for the main building in BMW's complex in Leipzig, Germany, was constructed, cars rolling on a conveyor belt past the office workers. At the London Olympics in 2012, her aquatic centre was an architectural centrepiece, the design inspired by water, with a swooping wave of a roof. And her exploration of fluid shapes went further still that same year, with the opening of a cultural centre in Azerbaijan, its white, flowing form described by architect Piers Gough as being 'as pure and sexy as Marilyn's blown skirt'.

Hadid was born in Baghdad, Iraq, in 1950. Her father Muhammad was co-founder of the National Democratic Party, and her mother Wajiha stayed at home and taught her daughter to draw. This was an optimistic, progressive era,

Hadid always said, in which girls in Iraq were expected to grow up to be professionals, and religious divisions weren't obviously apparent (Hadid didn't realise she was a Muslim until she was six, when the nuns at her convent school asked her to make the sign of the cross). From a young age she had an inkling that she would become an architect. The desire was triggered by an architectural model that appeared in her living room one day, a plan for a house her aunt was building in Mosul. She was also inspired by a visit, as a teenager, to Sumer in the south of Iraq, where the first cities in history were built.

After attending boarding schools in the UK and Switzerland, she went to study maths at the American University in Beirut. Then it was on to London and the Architectural Association, where she began painting her explosive visions. She was deeply influenced by the Constructivist movement that had emerged in Russia in the 1910s, which considered art to have an intrinsic social purpose. In an interview in the *Guardian* in 2006, she said she would love to build, 'schools, hospitals, social housing. Of course I believe imaginative architecture can make a difference to people's lives, but I wish it was possible to divert some of the effort we put into ambitious museums and galleries into the basic architectural building blocks of society'. Her design for the Evelyn Grace Academy, a school in Brixton, won the 2011 Stirling Prize.

Hadid was criticised for undertaking projects in countries and for regimes with questionable human rights records – her work on the Azerbaijan cultural centre attracted particular criticism. When asked by Young whether this concerned her when she was embarking on a new project, Hadid said, 'It does. But I think if you're doing a cultural building for the people it's a very different story than doing something else . . . I think it's very important in any of these countries that you actually contribute culturally in a positive way to that place. Because there will be no change anywhere if there isn't that element.'

When Hadid died in 2016, fewer than a quarter of the architects working in Britain were women, but she showed it could be done, becoming the first woman to win the Pritzker Prize in 2004, and the first in her own right to be awarded the RIBA Royal Gold Medal the year before she died.

In the citation for the RIBA award, architect Peter Cook wrote, 'if Paul Klee took a line for a walk, then Zaha took the surfaces that were driven by that line out for a virtual dance and then deftly folded them over and then took them out for a journey into space'. Her older brothers had wanted her to be Iraq's first woman astronaut, and Hadid was, after all, her own planet. She was once asked why it had taken so long for her plans to be built. 'I don't think people believed in the fantastic,' she said.

Lee Miller

Photojournalist, 1907–1977

Lee Miller in the bath at Adolf Hitler's abandoned
home in Munich, Germany, 1945.

> **'I would rather take a picture than be one'**

'I got in over my head. I could never get the stench of Dachau out of my nostrils,' Lee Miller told her biographer Carolyn Burke in 1977. She was the only female photojournalist to have seen combat during the Second World War, one of the first to reach Dachau and Buchenwald concentration camps, and she also took images of Germans killed by their own hand, and the firing squad execution of László Bárdossy, former Hungarian prime minister. After the war, her self-medication for what would now likely be considered post-traumatic stress disorder included benzedrine and bitter coffee in the morning, alcohol and sleeping pills before bed. She couldn't work, and a 1949 visit to her doctor must have suggested no escape. 'There is nothing wrong with you,' he said, 'and we cannot keep the world permanently at war just to provide you with entertainment.'

Antony Penrose, her son, called his biography *The Lives of Lee Miller*, a nod to her incarnations: model, muse, high society photographer, actor and surrealist chef. What seems to have driven her during the war, her most productive period, was her need for people to face the truth, however confronting.

There is no place in polite society for survivors to describe their experiences, and Miller would take her earliest trauma to the grave, hidden from her son and her husband Roland. She was born in Poughkeepsie, New York, in 1907, and when she was seven was raped by a family friend, contracting gonorrhoea. There began excruciating treatment; the equipment her mother Florence used included a glass catheter and rubber tubing, and Miller's screaming was so loud her brothers were sent two blocks away to protect them.

After the rape, 'she went wild', her older brother John once said, expelled from school after school. In 1925, aged eighteen, she travelled to Paris, studying stage design; arriving back in Poughkeepsie the next year, the town couldn't hold her. She moved to New York to study art.

The moment she was discovered as a model sounds apocryphal. Stumbling into traffic, she was pulled to safety by Condé Nast, founder of the publishing empire that included *Vogue*. The magazine was looking for models who personified modernity, and – slightly androgynous, slightly wild – she was perfect. On the March 1927 cover, in an illustration by Georges Lepape, Miller appears in a cloche hat, against a sea of city lights, eyes hard, jaw strong, neck knotted with pearls.

She looked like an angel, 'but I was a fiend inside,' Miller said later. When her image was used to advertise sanitary pads she was outraged, writes Burke, then pleased at having shocked her friends and family. She was becoming well known, but New York couldn't contain her either. She returned to France in 1929, 'to enter photography by the back end', behind the camera.

Miller went to Man Ray's Montparnasse studio, determined the renowned photographer would be her tutor. 'He said he didn't take students,' she said later, 'and anyway he was leaving Paris for his holiday. I said, I know, I'm going with you – and I did.' They became lovers, and soon she was apprenticing at *French Vogue* under chief of photography, George Hoyningen-Huene, forming a trio with fellow apprentice, Horst.

One day, turning on the lights too soon in the darkroom she shared with Ray, she discovered the technique now known as solarization, a startling, dynamic over-exposure. Ray's solarized portrait of Miller in profile became one of his best known photographs, and he also created surrealist portraits of her during their relationship, and after it ended in 1932. His painting *Observatory Time: The Lovers* (1936) shows her lips in the sky, floating above a forest.

She pursued surrealism too. Working at the Sorbonne medical school, she took a breast removed during a mastectomy, arranged it on a dinner plate, and photographed it. She also performed in the classic Jean Cocteau film *The Blood of a Poet* (1930), as a statue who comes to life.

After her relationship with Ray ended, she returned to New York, becoming the photographer everyone wanted to sit for. *Vanity Fair* called her one of the seven 'most distin-guished living photographers'. But she was still restless. In 1934 she married Aziz Eloui Bey, an Egyptian businessman almost two decades her senior, and moved to Cairo; in 1937, bored, she decided to summer with the Surrealists in Paris. There she met British artist Roland Penrose, and their love affair began. Pablo Picasso painted six portraits of her that summer.

Come 1939, she was living with Penrose in London, and on being accredited as a war reporter, it wasn't just her images that proved startling, but her prose too. Audrey

Withers, editor of *British Vogue*, described publishing her reportage as 'the most exciting journalistic experience of my war,' and when it came to work, Miller was all in. Still married to Bey, she wrote a guilty letter to her parents when news reached her that he was sick: 'selfishly I don't want to lose the grasp I have on work at the moment – I couldn't pick up another chance, and work is what I need for the rest of my life.'

The evening of her trip to Dachau, her friend and lover Dave Scherman photographed her in Adolf Hitler's bathtub – they had found refuge in the dictator's abandoned house. This became perhaps the most famous image of her. In the years to come, she married Roland, had Antony when she was 40, and developed her growing devotion to cookery. At the family home in Sussex, Farley Farm, she entertained guests with 'Surrealist surprises', including pink cauliflower breasts.

Miller 'abhorred manacles, whether political, social or domestic,' her friend, journalist Bettina McNulty, once said. Had her unhappiness been well treated, not dismissed, her last three decades might have been as productive as her first four. But still, she made us look, to acknowledge the horror when this was most needed, despite the unbearable cost to herself. After her death, more than 60,000 photographs and negatives were found in the attic at Farley Farm, testament to her unflinching eye.

Nina Simone

Musician, 1933–2003

Nina Simone, October 1969.

> *'I started to think of myself as a black person in a country run by white people and a woman in a world run by men'*

She had decided to build a gun. In September 1963, a church in Birmingham, Alabama was bombed by the Ku Klux Klan, killing four African-American girls, and injuring 22 other people. On hearing this, Nina Simone went to her garage and 'got a load of tools and junk together . . .' she wrote in her 1991 autobiography, *I Put a Spell on You*. 'I was trying to make a zip gun, a home-made pistol. I had it in my mind to go out and kill someone'. When her husband found her, he watched a while, before saying 'Nina, you don't know anything about killing. The only thing you've got is music'.

An hour later, she had written her first civil rights song, 'Mississippi Goddam'. 'Alabama's got me so upset,' it began, 'Tennessee made me lose my rest, and everybody knows about Mississippi Goddam.' This last was a reference to the June 1963 murder of Medgar Evers, a civil rights activist, by a member of the White Citizens' Council, a group set up to resist the integration of schools. The song was driving, emphatic, and brought the house down, again and again. A crate of records, all snapped in half, was sent back from a dealer in South Carolina, and there were problems with distribution in the South. This was said to be because of the profanity. Simone knew better.

'For the next seven years,' she writes, 'I was driven by civil rights and the hope of black revolution,' and she wrote and performed extraordinary, enduring political songs. Images, set to lyrics by Harlem Renaissance poet, William Waring Cuney, begins: 'she does not know her beauty / she thinks her brown body has no glory'. 'Four Women' traced the legacy of slavery and racism – 'my father was rich and white / he forced my mother late one night' – and also colorism, an idea defined by author Alice Walker in 1982, which recognises discrimination based on the specific shade of a person's skin, rather than simply their race.

'Backlash Blues' had lyrics by poet Langston Hughes (who, along with writer James Baldwin, mentored Simone); and when civil rights leader Martin Luther King Jr was assassinated in Memphis, Tennessee on 4 April 1968, Simone's double bass player Gene Taylor wrote 'Why? (The King of Love is Dead)'. Then there was the song which became known as the National Anthem of Black America, written in memory of Simone's friend, playwright Lorraine Hansberry, who wrote the enormously successful 'A Raisin in the Sun' while still in her twenties. The pair would talk about 'Marx, Lenin and revolution', and after Hansberry died of cancer at 34, Simone wrote a song with the same title as the play she had been working on: 'To Be Young, Gifted and Black'.

Born Eunice Waymon in North Carolina in 1933, Simone surprised everyone as an infant – not yet three – by playing one of her mother's favourite hymns on the pedal organ. Her mother was a Methodist preacher, and it was decided Simone had a gift from god. By six she was the pianist at the local church, and soon her lessons were being paid for by Mrs Miller, a white woman who employed Simone's mother as a housekeeper. Tutored by Muriel Massinovitch, she played only Bach at first, preparing to become the first black American concert pianist.

At a recital when she was eleven, she spoke out about racism from the stage when she saw her parents being moved from the front row to make way for a white family. She would not play if they were moved, she said, and noticed some of the white people laughing. Afterwards, she felt as if she had been flayed, she wrote, 'but the skin grew back again a little tougher, a little less innocent, and a little more black'.

Her home town of Tryon clubbed together for her tuition, and she went to boarding school, where piano practice began at 4am; she graduated as valedictorian. A year training at Juilliard was supposed to lead to her winning a full scholarship to the Curtis Institute of Music in Philadelphia, and the pressure was immense. She carried the hopes of her race; the investment of her hometown; and the expectations of her family, who moved to Philadelphia, sure she would succeed. She was rejected. Simone came to believe this was because of racism, and as she wrote, the insidious nature of discrimination is that 'you feel the shame, humiliation and anger at being just another victim of prejudice and at the same time there's the nagging worry that maybe it isn't that at all, maybe it's because you're just no good'.

She started playing in a seedy bar in Atlantic City, changing her name to Nina Simone to keep this secret from her mother. Dressed in a long, chiffon gown, she refused to play if people were speaking, closing her eyes, pretending she was at Carnegie Hall. 'Simone was able to conjure glamour in spite of everything the world said about black women who looked like her,' Ta-Nehisi Coates has written. 'And for that she enjoyed a special place in the pantheon of resistance.' Her voice, low and pregnant with emotion, mesmerised audiences.

Soon she was playing in Greenwich Village, and became a star – signing away many of her royalties in the first flush of success. She married a police detective, Andrew Stroud, who became her manager, and was physically violent; they had a child, Lisa Celeste, to whom Simone was physically abusive; she blazed through the civil rights era, targeted with death threats; and after her marriage ended she moved to Barbados, Liberia, Switzerland, then France. It is thought that Simone had bipolar disorder, and in her later years she lived through a suicide attempt and much else. She was found naked in a hotel corridor, carrying a knife; she shot and missed a record producer who she said owed her royalties; and she injured a French teenager, who she said had disturbed her music practice, shooting him in the leg with a pellet gun.

In the late 1980s, her song 'My Baby Just Cares For Me' was used in a Chanel advertisement, and her star rose again. 'Every generation has to discover Nina Simone,' Germaine Greer once said. 'She is evidence that female genius is real.' This was echoed by Angela Davis. 'In representing all of the women who had been silenced,' Davis has written, 'in sharing her incomparable artistic genius, she was the embodiment of the revolutionary democracy we had not yet learned how to imagine.'

Helen Keller

Author and activist, 1880–1968

Helen Keller reading a book in braille, 1950.

Helen Keller had two birthdays. The first was 27 June 1880, when she was born in the rural town of Tuscumbia, Alabama. The second was her 'soul's birthday', 3 March 1887, when her teacher Annie Sullivan arrived at her home. Sullivan gave her deaf and blind pupil the gift of language, and Keller used this with aplomb. She wrote books and letters, gave hundreds of lectures, campaigned for women's suffrage and against racism, and emerged as perhaps the best known disability rights campaigner of all time.

Keller lost her hearing and sight when she was nineteen months old, to an illness now thought to have been either scarlet fever or meningitis. As a small child, she was given to temper tantrums, pinching and biting relatives, breaking plates, throwing food, and overturning the cot of her younger sister Mildred (who thankfully survived). Her parents contacted what is now the Perkins School for the Blind, to ask for help, and its director agreed to send his star graduate, Annie Sullivan, who had grown up with a visual impairment herself.

Born into extreme poverty to Irish immigrants in 1866, Sullivan developed trachoma, an infection that can cause blindness, aged five, lost her mother to tuberculosis when she was eight, and was abandoned by her physically abusive father aged ten. She and her younger brother Jimmie, who was five, then entered the poorhouse; as Dorothy Herrmann notes in her biography of Keller, not one of the other 27 foundling children who arrived at the poorhouse that same year survived, in an environment where rats roamed freely and infectious diseases were rife. Three months later, Jimmie died. After viewing his corpse, Sullivan wrote, 'I went out quietly, I sat down beside my bed and wished to die with an intensity that I have never wished for anything else'.

She spent four years in the poorhouse, before transferring to the Perkins School aged fourteen, where she graduated first in her class. She also had two operations on her eyes, which left her sight blurry, but enabled her to read. The trip to Tuscumbia must have been daunting – Sullivan would be hundreds of miles from anyone she knew – but it was a job, at $25 a month, and she grabbed the opportunity.

Not long after she arrived, Keller, wild as ever, knocked out one of Sullivan's front teeth. Then everything changed. Sullivan placed her hand under a water spout one day, Keller writes in *The Story of My Life*, and, 'as the cool stream gushed over one hand she spelled into the other the word "water", first slowly, then rapidly. I stood still, my whole attention fixed upon the motions of her fingers. Suddenly I felt a misty consciousness as of something forgotten – a thrill of returning thought; and somehow the mystery of language was revealed to me. I knew then that "w-a-t-e-r" meant the wonderful cool something that was flowing over my hand. That living word awakened my soul, gave it light, hope, joy, set it free!'

Keller became the first deaf blind person to gain a Bachelor of Arts degree, graduating from Radcliffe at a time when very few women attended university. She was hailed as a genius – except when she expressed challenging views, at which point many people found it surprisingly easy to question her intelligence. In her late twenties, she began supporting the Socialist party and campaigned for workers' rights, and went on to join the union the Industrial Workers of the World. After being appointed to a commission to investigate the conditions of the blind, Keller remarked, 'for the first time I, who had thought blindness a misfortune beyond human control, found that too much of it was traceable to wrong industrial conditions, often caused by the selfishness and greed of employers'. Keller was keenly aware of privilege and class, and the ways people were exploited. 'Ever since childhood, my feelings have been with the slaves,' she once said.

She was at risk of exploitation herself. In her teenage years, while her father was alive, he threatened to address his financial problems by exhibiting her as a curiosity on the vaudeville circuit. Her mother Kate saw off this humiliation. But as Helen Keller reached her forties, facing financial problems herself, she and Sullivan took to the circuit, for an act including a question and answer session, addressing social and political issues. Vaudeville was a world of child performers, tattooed ladies and stunt men. It wasn't respectable. Keller liked it.

There were periods of melancholia in Keller's life, but she was also highly sociable. She attended the theatre regularly (the action was spelled into her hand), and met presidents and performers, from Franklin D. Roosevelt to Charlie Chaplin, becoming great friends with Mark Twain.

'If I could see,' said Keller, 'I would marry first of all.' She came close in her mid-thirties, when she applied for a marriage license with Peter Fagan, who shared her political views and had started working for her and Sullivan as their secretary. But the relationship was opposed by her mother and their plans fell through. Her closest relationship was with Sullivan, and lasted 49 years until Sullivan's death. It was a parting they had dreaded – Keller wrote a book in tribute afterwards, called *Teacher* – but she continued to have a full, adventurous life, travelling the world well into old age with her secretary and companion Polly Thomson, campaigning and fundraising for the blind. Keller's story has sometimes been used in a way she would surely have hated, to suggest disabled people should simply follow her example, work hard, succeed as individuals, pull themselves up by the boot straps. But she understood that certain problems were collective, structural and political, and dedicated her extraordinary life to solving them.

Claudia Jones

Writer and activist, 1915–1964

Claudia Jones arriving in Southampton, England from the US on the
ocean liner *Queen Elizabeth*, 1955.

> *'Let us rededicate ourselves to the fight for the complete equality of women'*

In 1955, Claudia Jones was deported from the United States – her home since childhood – to the United Kingdom. As a Caribbean woman, she wasn't entering a welcoming environment. Seven years earlier, the Empire Windrush had brought almost 500 Caribbean passengers to the UK, heralding a new wave of post-war migration, those on board promised jobs and a warm reception. For many, the reality was very different. The writer Donald Hinds described this era vividly in a 2008 essay. 'Landlords and landladies still advertised rooms for rent under the legend: "No Irish! No Coloureds!"' he wrote. There were regular calls for the control of black immigration, white bus passengers would jump from their seat if a black passenger sat beside them, many employers refused to hire black people, and some public houses refused to serve black customers.

Before her deportation, Jones had spent seven years in and out of jail in the US, detained for her Communist beliefs. Diagnosed with hypertensive cardiovascular disease, she suffered a heart attack not long before travelling to the UK, but on arrival in London, rather than resting, she immediately continued her life's work – organising against oppression.

Jones had been born in Trinidad, moved with her family to the US when she was eight, and in the UK found a Caribbean community that was growing quickly, and suffering significant racism. Two years after she arrived, she became founder-editor of *The West Indian Gazette*, the first major black newspaper in the UK (later *The West Indian Gazette and Afro-Asian Caribbean News*), whose offices were above a Caribbean record shop in Brixton. In the first issue, in March 1958, Jones wrote that, 'there are at least 80,000 good reasons why we believe a West Indian newspaper is necessary and will be welcomed. They are the 80,000-odd West Indians now resident here'.

In August 1958, violence spread through Notting Hill in west London, as nine young white men went hunting for black victims, with iron bars, an air pistol and a knife. Five black men ended up in hospital, three seriously hurt. A week later, 200 people marched through Notting Hill, carrying weapons and shouting 'Go home you black bastards'. West Indian residents fought back, the violence continuing for three days.

The community needed something to wash this taste out of their mouths, Jones decided; a carnival, in the Caribbean tradition. In January 1959, in St Pancras Town Hall, calypsonians, steel bands and carnival queens gathered for the event which would be the forerunner of the enormously popular Notting Hill Carnival. It was televised by BBC music programme 'Six-Five Special', and sponsored by *The West Indian Gazette*, the souvenir programme featuring Jones's essay, 'A People's Art is the Genesis of Their Freedom'. The carnival continued annually until her death of heart failure in 1964. In the wake of this tragedy, the next year's event was cancelled.

Now best known as mother of the Notting Hill Carnival, Jones's work as a writer and activist was extensive, and she formulated many of the ideas essential to what later became known as intersectional feminism. Her political consciousness can be traced, in part, to the death of her mother in 1933, while Jones was still at high school. In a 1955 letter, Jones wrote that her mother died 'of spinal meningitis suddenly at her machine in a garment shop. The conditions of non-union organisation . . . and undoubtedly the weight of immigration to a new land where conditions were far from as promised or anticipated, contributed to her early death at 37'. Carole Boyce Davies writes in her political biography of Jones, *Left of Karl Marx*, that the family's economic difficulties may also have contributed to Jones's ill health later in life. 'An open sewer flowed past their apartment;' writes Davies, 'the poor housing conditions clearly led to her contracting tuberculosis and being hospitalised in a New York sanatorium at the age of seventeen.'

In her early twenties, she was employed in laundry and factory work, and became involved in organising around the Scottsboro Boys case – nine young black men who were falsely accused of raping two white women. Despite medical evidence suggesting their innocence, all were sentenced to death except one twelve-year-old defendant. The Communist Party organised in their defence, and Jones became a party member.

She worked as a journalist, starting the column Claudia's Comments for a black newspaper in 1935, and a decade later became Negro Affairs editor for the Daily Worker. In the early 1950s, her Daily Worker column, Half the World, addressed women's issues.

Two of her most influential, enduring essays were published in 1949: We Seek Full Equality for Women, and An End to the Neglect of the Problems of the Negro Woman! In the first she writes that 'the triply-oppressed status of Negro women is a barometer of the status of all women', and in the second, that 'degradation and super-exploitation: this is the actual lot of Negro women!' before describing how that super-exploitation plays out in fields such as domestic work. Her analysis recognised acutely how race, sex and class intersected to define women's lives and opportunities.

FBI surveillance of Jones began in 1942, and Davies writes that her file was eventually almost a thousand pages long. But despite the McCarthyite hysteria of the period, and the determined targeting of Communists, the authorities apparently found it difficult to construct a case against Jones. They were reliant on 'literary evidence', trying to use her writing against her, writes Davies, but 'there was no factual evidence that she or her comrades were in any way involved in overthrowing the US government by force, as was charged. In some cases, Jones's FBI file itself spoke to this absence of evidence, asking its agents to seek out more revolutionary statements, as all the state had for its case was a collection of essays on the need for the equality of black people and women'.

Despite the dearth of evidence, they imprisoned then deported her. Many would have been broken by a forced journey to a new country, but in her final years in the UK – as the legacy of carnival proves – Jones was irrepressible.

Ana Mendieta

Artist, 1948–1985

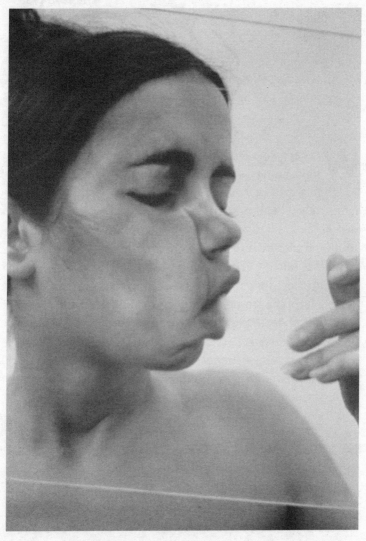

Self-portrait photograph by Ana Mendieta, *Untitled* (6 works, from the Glass on Body Imprints), 1972

> **'My art is the way I reestablish the bonds that tie me to the universe'**

Where is Ana Mendieta? The question has been asked many times since the artist's shocking death, aged 36 – subject of protests, pleas, a book, an exhibition and a symposium – and pertains as much to her work as her life. Mendieta is such a compelling presence when she does appear in photos and videos, that her niece, Raquel Cecilia Mendieta, has described her surprise, while compiling and restoring her aunt's 104 films, at how quickly she disappeared from the frame of her own work. Often described as a performance artist – one of many categories Mendieta shrugged off – she only appears in 37 of her own videos, with the last, *Black Ixchell, Candle Ixchell* (1977), showing her lying down, wrapped and bound in a black shroud, a lighted candle balanced on her chest.

When Mendieta made this work, she was halfway through her most extensive series, the *Siluetas* (1973–1980). This began in Mexico, 'in an Aztec tomb that was covered with weeds and grasses,' Mendieta once said. 'I bought flowers at the market, lay in the tomb and was covered with white flowers. The analogy was that I was covered by time and history.'

What she called 'earth-body' works had begun, but Mendieta tended not to appear in them. Instead, the image captured on camera was of her silhouette, sculpted in snow; imprinted in sand; forming the centre of a volcano. Hans Breder, her lover and tutor at the University of Iowa, sometimes traced these silhouettes directly around her body; in one untitled 1974 work, for instance, she lay down at an archeological site in Oaxaca, Mexico, Breder traced her shape, she created a rim around the resulting silhouette, and filled it with blood from a local butcher. On other occasions, a template of her body was used to make the work. Joanna S. Walker has described the first piece made this way, *Ánima Silueta de Cohetes* (1976), consisting, 'of a wood and rope frame of her body . . . Mendieta positioned fireworks around this frame, which she set alight against the background of a night sky. The rapid explosion of the firework effigy is captured by both photography and Super-8 film'. More than a hundred *Siluetas* were made, documented, then left to the elements. The absent woman in these images, often posed with her arms up – an iconic goddess or robber caught red handed – evokes memory, loss and the quicksilver passage of time.

The silhouettes also evoke crime scene outlines. In 1985, when Mendieta's reputation was growing, a doorman heard a woman shout 'No, no, no, no' and the artist fell from her 34th-floor apartment in Greenwich Village, New York, landing on the delicatessen roof below. Mendieta's husband, renowned minimalist sculptor Carl Andre called the emergency services, and told them, 'My wife is an artist, and I'm an artist, and we had a quarrel about the fact that I was more, eh, exposed to the public than she was. And she went to the bedroom, and I went after her, and she went out the window'. When the police arrived, they found scratches on Andre's arm and face.

He was charged with murder, and many of his art world associates came to his defence. At the end of an unusual trial – the case heard by a judge but no jury – Andre was acquitted. Mendieta's friends were devastated by her death, and when Andre's work was included at an exhibition at the Guggenheim Museum SoHo in 1992, around 500 protesters gathered, their banners reading: 'Where is Ana Mendieta?'

The artist's sister, Raquelin Mendieta, has warned against viewing her work through the prism of her death, saying her art is, instead, 'about life and power and energy'. The sisters were close, exiled together in adolescence. The Mendieta family was powerful in their home country, Cuba – the sisters' great uncle Carlos was President in 1934 – but when Fidel Castro came to power in 1959, their father Ignacio became involved in counter–revolutionary activities, and Ana, twelve, and Raquelin, fifteen, were sent to live in the United States for their own safety. They ended up in Iowa, in a Catholic orphanage that was essentially a reform school. It was five years before they saw their mother and brother again; eighteen years before they saw their father.

At high school, Mendieta decided to be an artist, and when teachers told her she was untalented, she said she didn't care. She became a painting major at the University of Iowa, where the Intermedia department, founded by Breder, was highly influential. Soon she began experimenting. Blood became a notable material; the film *Sweating Blood* (1973), shows drops of it rolling slowly down her face.

In March 1973, a nursing student at the University of Iowa was raped and murdered, and Mendieta started a short series of work in response. In the first piece, *Untitled (Rape*

Scene), she invited students to her apartment, where they found the door ajar, and Mendieta inside, naked from the waist down, smeared with blood, bent over a table to which her head and hands were tied. The students 'all sat down,' Mendieta said later, 'and started talking about it. I didn't move. I stayed in position about an hour. It really jolted them.' In *Untitled (People Looking at Blood, Moffitt)*, she photographed people walking by a pile of animal viscera and blood she'd deposited on the pavement outside her apartment.

Mendieta is sometimes described as a feminist artist, and in 1978 she joined the pioneering A.I.R. Gallery in New York, run by women artists, to showcase their work. She met Andre there, when he appeared on a panel regarding women's art and the social attitudes of male artists, but in 1982 resigned from the gallery. 'American feminism as it stands,' she once said, 'is basically a white middle class movement.'

As an artist, she was determined to defy categorisation, to represent something more elemental. Her art was grounded, she wrote, 'on the belief in one universal energy which runs through everything: from insect to man, from man to spectre, from spectre to plant, from plant to galaxy'.

INDEX

SELECT BIBLIOGRAPHY

In her 1929 essay 'A Room of One's Own', Virginia Woolf outlines the case for rewriting history to include women; looking along her bookshelves, she writes, 'one often catches a glimpse of them in the lives of the great, whisking away into the background, concealing, I sometimes think, a wink, a laugh, perhaps a tear'. Thankfully, if Woolf entered a library today, she would find a revolution on the shelves, writers investigating, reclaiming and retelling the stories of women – including their own. If that revolution had not happened, this book would have been impossible.

Abrams, Fran. *Freedom's Cause: Lives of the Suffragettes*, Profile Books, 2003

Acker, Ally. *Reel Women: Pioneers of the Cinema*, Vol.I 1890s-1950s, Reel Women Media Publishing, 2012

Adams, Jad. *Women & the Vote: A World History*, Oxford University Press, 2014

Adichie, Chimamanda Ngozi. *We Should All Be Feminists*, Fourth Estate, 2014

Anand, Anita. *Sophia: Princess, Suffragette, Revolutionary*, Bloomsbury Publishing, 2015

Angelou, Maya. *I Know Why the Caged Bird Sings*, Virago Press, 1984

Angelou, Maya. *Letter to my Daughter*, Virago Press, 2009

Ball, Lucille. *Love, Lucy*, G.P. Putnam's Sons, 1996

Bay, Mia. *To Tell the Truth Freely: The Life of Ida B. Wells*, Hill and Wang, 2009

Britton, Andrew. *Katharine Hepburn: Star as Feminist*, Studio Vista, 1995

Burke, Carolyn. *Lee Miller*, Bloomsbury Publishing, 2005

Butler, Susan. *East to the Dawn: The Life of Amelia Earhart*, Da Capo Press, 1999

Chadwick, Whitney. *Women, Art and Society*, Thames & Hudson Ltd, 2012 edition

Clinton, Catherine. *Harriet Tubman: The Road to Freedom*, Little, Brown and Company, 2004

Davies, Carole Boyce. *Left of Karl Marx: the Political Life of Claudia Jones*, Duke University Press, 2008

Dumbach, Annette & Newborn, Jud. *Sophie Scholl and the White Rose*, Oneworld Publications, 2006 edition

Ebadi, Shirin. *Iran Awakening: One Woman's Journey to Reclaim Her Life and Country*, Random House, 2007

Ebadi, Shirin. *Until we are Free: My Fight for Human Rights in Iran*, Rider, 2016

Ephron, Nora. *Crazy Salad: Some Things About Women & Scribble Scribble: Notes on the Media*, Vintage Books edition, 2012

Ephron, Nora. *The Most of Nora Ephron*, Doubleday, 2014

Essinger, James. *A Female Genius: How Ada Lovelace, Lord Byron's Daughter, Started the Computer Age*, Gibson Square, 2014

Faderman, Lillian. *Odd Girls and Twilight Lovers: A History of Lesbian Life in 20th Century America*, Columbia University Press, 2012

Freedman, Russell. *Martha Graham: A Dancer's Life*, Clarion Books, 1998

Gbowee, Leymah (with Mithers, Carol). *Mighty Be Our Powers: A Memoir*, Beast Books, 2011

Gee, Christine; Weare, Garry; and Gee, Margaret (Eds). *Everest: Reflections from the Top*, Rider, 2003

Graham, Martha. *Blood Memory: An Autobiography*, Doubleday, 1991

Greer, Germaine. *The Obstacle Race*, Martin Secker & Warburg Limited, 1979

Gordon, Charlotte. *Romantic Outlaws: The Extraordinary Lives of Mary Wollstonecraft & Mary Shelley*, Windmill Books, 2016

Gordon, Linda. *Dorothea Lange: A Life Beyond Limits*, WW Norton & Company, 2009

Guerrilla Girls. *Confessions of the Guerrilla Girls*, HarperCollins Publishers, 1995

Guy-Blaché, Alice. *The Memoirs of Alice Guy-Blaché*, translated by Roberta and Simone Blaché, Scarecrow Press, 1996

Heilbrun, Carolyn. *The Education of a Woman: The Life and Times of Gloria Steinem*, Virago Press, 1996

Hepburn, Katharine. *Me: Stories of my Life*, Ballantine Books, 1991

Herrera, Hayden. *Frida: the Biography of Frida Kahlo*, Bloomsbury Publishing, 2003 edition

Herrmann, Dorothy. *Helen Keller: A Life*, Alfred A Knopf, 1998

Isaacson, Walter. *The Innovators: How a Group of Hackers, Geniuses and Geeks Created the Digital Revolution*, Simon & Schuster UK, 2014

Keller, Helen. *The Story of my Life*, Bantam Classic edition, 2005

Lee, Hermione. *Virginia Woolf*, Vintage, 1997

Lorde, Audre. *Zami: A New Spelling of my Name*, Persephone Press, 1982

Lorde, Audre. *I Am Your Sister: Collected and Unpublished Writings of Audre Lorde*, Oxford University Press, 2009

Lorde, Audre. *Sister Outsider*, The Crossing Press feminist series, 2007

Maathai, Wangari. *Unbowed: One Woman's Story*, William Heinemann, 2007

Maddox, Brenda. *Rosalind Franklin: The Dark Lady of DNA*, HarperCollins Publishers, 2002

Mahar, Karen Ward. *Women Filmmakers in Early Hollywood*, The Johns Hopkins University Press, 2006

Maitland, Sara. *Vesta Tilley*, Virago Press, 1986

Makeba, Miriam. *Makeba: My Story*, Bloomsbury Publishing, 1988

Mann, William J. *Kate: The Woman who was Katharine Hepburn*, Henry Holt and Company, 2006

Manton, Jo. *Elizabeth Garrett Anderson: England's First Woman Physician*, Methuen, 1965

Marcus, Sara. *Girls to the Front: The True Story of the Riot Grrrl Revolution*, Harper Perennial, 2010

Marlow, Joyce. *Suffragettes: The Fight for Votes for Women*, Virago, 2015

Morris, Jan. *Conundrum*, Faber and Faber Limited, 1974

Morris, Jan. *Pleasures of a Tangled Life*, Barrie & Jenkins Ltd, 1989

Nolen, Stephanie, *Promised the Moon: The Untold Story of the First Women in the Space Race*, Four Walls Eight Windows, 2003

Nyad, Diana. *Find a Way*, Alfred A Knopf, 2015

Nyad, Diana. *Other Shores*, Random House, 1978

Pierce, Patricia. *Jurassic Mary: Mary Anning and the Primeval Monsters*, The History Press, 2014 edition

Reckitt, Helena (Ed). *Art and Feminism*, Phaidon Press, 2001

Rhimes, Shonda. *The Year of Yes*, Simon & Schuster UK Ltd, 2015

Simone, Nina (with Cleary, Stephen). *I Put a Spell on You: The Autobiography of Nina Simone*, Da Capo Press, 1993

Slide, Anthony. *The Silent Feminists: America's First Women Directors*, Scarecrow Press, 1996

Smith, Maureen M. *Wilma Rudolph: A Biography*, Greenwood Press, 2006

Smith, Sharon. *Women Who Make Movies*, Hopkinson and Blake, 1975

Steinem, Gloria. *Moving Beyond Words*, Simon & Schuster, 1994

Steinem, Gloria. *My Life on the Road*, Oneworld Publications, 2015

Tereshkova, Valentina. 'The First Lady of Space: In Her Own Words', SpaceHistory101.com Press, 2015 (reprinted with the permission of the journal *Quest: The History of Spaceflight Quarterly*)

Thom, Mary. *Inside Ms: 25 Years of the Magazine and the Feminist Movement*, Henry Holt and Company, 1997

Watson, James. *The Double Helix*, Weidenfeld & Nicolson, 1968

Woolf, Virginia. 'A Room of One's Own', Penguin Classics edition, 2000

ACKNOWLEDGEMENTS

This project began with Nicki Davis and Anna Watson at Frances Lincoln sending over the beautiful pages they'd put together to illustrate their idea for a book about women pioneers. Throughout this process, Nicki has been an incredibly patient, kind and perceptive editor, and Anna's photo research has been brilliant too. I couldn't have hoped to work with a better team.

For more than a decade now I've been lucky enough to work with one of the pioneers of British journalism, Katharine Viner, the first woman editor of the *Guardian*, a great inspiration. I'm also very grateful for the other excellent women I've worked with in newspaper offices over the years, including Sarah Baxter, Eleanor Mills, Sue Matthias, Homa Khaleeli, Paula Cocozza, Katherine Butler, Sarah Phillips, Emily Wilson, Clare Margetson, Maya Wolfe-Robinson, Bella Mackie, Vicky Frost, Natalie Hanman, Becky Gardiner, Hannah Pool, Hannah Jane Parkinson, Jane Martinson, Emine Saner, Anne Perkins, Polly Toynbee, Zoe Williams, Marina Hyde, Hadley Freeman and Amy Fleming.

Thanks to all my colleagues on the Opinion desk at the *Guardian* for buoying me along, and to Simon Hattenstone, Mark Atkins, Jason Deans, Fanny Johnstone, Colin Midson, Emily Compton, Finnian Brewer and Jo Shapcott for their encouragement. Thanks too, to Lara Bove Vadell, for keeping me sane in the gym. And also to Matthew Hamilton for all his excellent help and advice.

Finally, thanks to Tessa and Frazer Cochrane, the best family anyone could have in a crisis, and beyond.

PICTURE CREDITS